# Discov(

## the

# HISTORY of BRITTANY

## by

# Wendy Mewes

with drawings by
Steve Leighton

a RED DOG book

Discovering the History of Brittany
published by Red Dog Books
ISBN 0 9536001 5 7

© Wendy Mewes 2006

**For
G Le P**

.

British Library Cataloguing-in-Publication Data
A catalogue record for this book is available from the British Library

Drawings © Steve Leighton

Red Dog Books is based in Axbridge, Somerset and in Brittany.
Enquiries should be addressed to the editorial office at
Red Dog Books, 29410 Plounéour-Ménez, France.

email: reddogbooks@tiscali.fr

www.reddogbooks.com

Printed and bound in China

Cover photo: Château de Kerouzéré, Sibiril, Finistère

## AUTHOR'S NOTE

The purpose of this book is to present a clear and concise account of the history of Brittany. It is intended for any English-speaking residents, visitors or tourists who would like a straightforward chronological framework against which to interpret the historical remains to be found in this remarkable region. History, of course, is not straightforward, and Brittany's past is a tapestry of particularly complex weave, with Celts, Britons, Vikings, Franks, French, English and Germans all contributing their threads to the pattern.

My endeavour has been to simplify without distortion and, where selectivity was essential, to choose events or episodes on the basis of visible legacies, as these are likely to be of major interest to the general reader. The cited examples range widely geographically, and include a deliberate mix of famous and less well-known places: it has been my experience that any corner of Brittany will repay exploration with a cornucopia of historical interest.

## ABOUT THE AUTHOR

Wendy Mewes studied at the University of Wales and University College London and has a research degree in ancient history. She taught this subject, together with Latin, for nearly twenty years, latterly as Head of Classics at Godolphin & Latymer in Hammersmith. After a spell in Somerset, she now lives in Brittany, in the department of Finistère. Her previous publications include *Finistère: Things to see and do at the End of the World (2004)*, *Walking and other activities in Finistère (2005)* and a novel, *Moon Garden*. See www.reddogbooks.com for further information.

## Acknowledgments

Special thanks to:-

Steve Leighton for his excellent illustrations

Francis Favereau for his helpful comments on
the manuscript

Bruno de Calan for permission to feature the
Château de Kerouzéré on the front cover

Isabelle Berthou-Bray at the Bibliothèque Bretonne,
Landévennec Abbey, for her kindness and expertise

Anne Guilliou of the Centre Culturel de Luzec, for some
timely help and an instinct for inspiration

Bibliothèque 'Les Amours Jaunes' in Morlaix

The many Breton historians from whose books, ideas and
talk I have learnt so much, and all our Breton friends and
neighbours who have shaped my commitment to the past,
present and future of Brittany

## PHOTOGRAPHS

# CONTENTS

Chapter                                                          page

**INTRODUCTION: WAYS & MEANS**
Types of evidence                                                  7

**CHRONOLOGICAL TABLE**                                           12

1   **MEN & STONES (c.5000 - 700BC)**
    Neolithic man - remains - religion -
    death & burial - dolmens - cairns -
    menhirs                                                       13

2   **CELTS & ROMANS (c.700BC - AD400)**
    tribes - social & political structure -
    settlements - religion - Roman administration
    towns & communications - civilisation -
    end of Roman rule                                             26

3   **DEPARTURES & ARRIVALS (c.400 - 799)**
    Dark Ages - legends - immigration -
    Christianity - Conomor - the Franks -
    the Carolingians                                              36

4   **KINGS & VIKINGS (799 - 952)**
    Morvan - Nominoë - Vikings -
    kings of Brittany - Alain Barbetorte -
    Landévennec Abbey                                             48

5   **DUKES & A DUCHESS (952 - 1514)**
    Early dukes - Plantagenet interest -
    House of Dreux - wars of succession -
    Montforts - François II - Anne de Bretagne   60

6   **UNION & PROSPERITY (1514 - 1673)**
    Union with France - wars of religion -
    trade & exploration - demands of Louis XIV   73

7   **UNREST & REVOLUTION (1673 - 1802)**
    Bonnets Rouges - Vauban - trade & ports -
    l'affaire de Bretagne - French Revolution -
    the Chouans - Napoleon                                        83

8    **WHITES & BLUES (1802 - 1914)**
     Napoleonic Brittany - political parties -
     restoration - republic & empire -
     communications - agriculture & industry -
     the Church - Breton movements          97

9    **WARS & BEYOND (1914 ...)**
     First World War - inter-war years -
     occupation & resistance - post-war
     reconstruction - economic development -
     Breton language - recent times          108

     **APPENDIX:**
     A Selection of Authors                  120

     **BIBLIOGRAPHY**                        123

     **INDEX**                               124

     **TABLE OF RULERS (BRITTANY & FRANCE)**  127

**MAPS**

**BRITTANY**                     inside front cover

**CELTIC TRIBES & ROMAN TOWNS**              27

**BRITTANY IN THE DARK AGES**                38

**BORDERS OF BRITTANY (9TH CENTURY)**        53

**MEDIEVAL BRITTANY**                        63

# INTRODUCTION - WAYS & MEANS

Evidence for the history of Brittany comes from many different sources, including primary records, which are contemporary with events they describe, and later secondary accounts. Written documents range from the personal to public and official records, and from literature to history, although all these are most often concerned with the interests and actions of the wealthier, more educated sections of society.

A closer glimpse of ordinary people often comes from material remains which cover a vast scale from small objects like coins, weapons, traditional costumes and furniture on the one hand, to huge structures like the megaliths and the grandest of public buildings on the other, and from the relics of ancient settlements to the extensive war-time coastal fortifications.

This short section presents a few of the main categories of evidence to illustrate its diversity and significance, sometimes overlooked in the modern age when any type of secondary information is readily accessible through books, newspapers, television and the internet.

## Archaeological Remains

Archaeology – evidence found through excavation – reveals much about life in periods before and after written evidence appears, but it also leaves many gaps in the knowledge and understanding of early society. Speculation and hypothesis from the basis of finds can nevertheless be useful, and the

process of discovery is a constant one.

There is an enormous variety of archaeological remains in Brittany - prehistoric sites such as standing stones and burial chambers, Roman villas, medieval settlements, monasteries and fortified châteaux are well-documented examples. Buildings provide evidence of local materials, engineering techniques and artistic decoration as well as giving an idea of domestic arrangements. The excavations at Corseul yielded enough information to enable an accurate reconstruction of a Roman street to be made, and the foundations of the colonnades, shops and dwellings remain in situ, an evocative exercise for the historic imagination.

## Artefacts
The objects found on such sites give further details of personal daily life: jewellery, tools and utensils, pottery and weapons rank among the commonest finds. There are also items like statuettes of gods and grave-goods which can give indications of religious beliefs and attitudes towards death and burial. Departmental museums all display fine examples, but there are also many local exhibitions of relevant finds.

## Coins
Coins warrant a mention separate from other artefacts. Earliest examples come from the Celtic tribes in Brittany and continue up to the modern euro. They have always been used to convey messages, particularly strong and important images in ages without other written forms of media. Coins are frequently vehicles of propaganda, presenting people (such as political leaders) in a particular way and transmitting symbols to a wide public on a currency often with daily usage.

## Inscriptions

This form of written evidence is immensely varied, from Roman votive offerings, describing who made them and why, to dedications on relatively modern tombstones giving a wealth of personal details (or a significant lack of detail, such as at the German war cemetery at Lesneven).

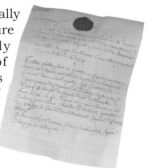

```
N.AVG.
NEPTVNO HIPPIO
C.VARENTIVS VOLTIN
VARVS C.C.R IIII
POSVIT
```

## Public Records

Purely factual records such as lists of office-holders and records of executive decisions provide accurate information about various aspects of local and regional government through the centuries.

There are also many other official documents such as French royal charters and Revolutionary decrees which relate to Breton history. Each department of Brittany has a rich store of this type of evidence in its archive offices.

The record-keeping of monasteries is also an invaluable source for early history. The Cartulaires of the Abbeys of Redon and Landévennec, listing resources and land-ownership over hundreds of years, contain a mass of detail about economic patterns, social organization, political history and nomenclature, as well as being works of art in their own right.

## Letters

Private documents like letters, especially those written without an eye to future publication, can be remarkably revealing of the personal detail of public events. The semi-official letters of the Duc de Chaulnes, governor of Brittany in the late 17th century, can be contrasted with the personal ones of those of his contemporary Madame de Sévigné.

## Histories

The writing of history becomes increasingly common from the early records of monks onwards, although there are also references to Brittany in the work of Julius Caesar himself from the Roman period. Medieval chroniclers such as Geoffrey of Monmouth, Froissart and Pierre Le Baud, a contemporary of Anne, Duchess of Brittany, provide many details of varying degrees of accuracy in terms of events and chronology. There is also the bias of the author to consider: Ernold Le Noir's 9th century accounts of Louis the Pious' incursions into Brittany are part of a work in honour of this king of the Franks.

## Biography and autobiography

An important category of biographies are those of the early Breton saints, such as Pol, Hervé and Gildas. Such works, a mixture of legend and fact, were written by monks, and their content remains a major source for early periods of Breton history. The same theme was also important for later writers, such as Albert Le Grand in the 17th century.

Many writers, both those born in Brittany and visitors to the region, have recorded their observations and experiences in a variety of works. Chateaubriand's autobiographical *Memoires d'outre-tombe* describes his childhood years growing up in the Château de Combourg. Guy de Maupassant in 1879 recorded his impression of the Château of Suscinio: "…there rose a tall ruin: a square castle, flanked with towers, standing there, all alone, between those two deserts: the moor and the sea… I was quite haunted in that old country; and I felt legends lurking in those walls, in the low, whistling gorse, in those stagnant ditches…"

## Novels

Works of the creative imagination also provide much of historical interest. Period particulars and authentic atmospheric details can be gleaned from novels as varied as Balzac's *The Chouans*, set in and around Fougères, about the anti-revolutionary movement in Brittany, and *Clauda Jegou* by Yves Le Febvre, a tragic tale of early 20th century peasant life in the Monts d'Arrée.

## Poetry

Poetry can be telling too in its subject matter, which often reflects major concerns of the period, or the revelation of its author's personality. Sharply contrasting examples would be the religious poetry of Pierre de Dreux, duke of Brittany in the early 13th century, and that of Tristan Corbière, a powerful avant garde poet born near Morlaix, who was writing more than six hundred years later.

## Oral traditions

A very different category of evidence is the strong oral tradition of Breton history. Songs, poems and legends record the people and events that caught the popular imagination, from the dastardly deeds of Conomor in the 6th century to the nuclear protests of the 1980s. The practice of transferring information from generation to generation by word of mouth in music and story-telling goes back at least to the Druidic traditions of the Celtic period and is still a strength of local culture today.

## Monuments

Numerous monuments all over Brittany are testimony to what was thought important in various ages, from streets named after WWII resistance fighters or marking the date of the ending of the Algerian War to statues showing historic figures. For example, Nominoë, for whom there is no known likeness, is nevertheless represented by a stylised statue because of his significance in Breton history. Simple plaques recording sites where individuals or many people lost their lives contrast with grand collective memorials of remembrance, such as that at Ste-Anne-d'Auray.

# CHRONOLOGICAL TABLE

**BC**

| | |
|---|---|
| c.5000 | Neolithic period |
| c.3000 | Carnac alignments |
| c.2000 | Bronze Age |
| c.700 | Iron Age - arrival of the Celts |
| from 56 | Roman administration of Armorica |

**AD**

| | |
|---|---|
| 4th cent. | British immigration begins |
| late 4th cent. | End of Roman administration |
| late 5th cent. | Peace with Clovis, king of the Franks |
| 800 | Charlemagne Holy Roman Emperor |
| c.831 | Nominoë 'missus imperatoris' |
| 843 | First Viking attack on Nantes |
| 851 | Erispoë acknowledged as King of Brittany |
| 913 | Landévennec Abbey sacked by Vikings |
| 939 | Major victory against the Vikings |
| 952 | Death of Alain Barbetorte, duke of Brittany |
| c.1160 | Plantagenet influence in Brittany |
| 1213 | Pierre de Dreux, French duke of Brittany |
| 1341 | Wars of Succession begin |
| 1364 | Montforts victorious |
| 1488 | Defeat of François II |
| 1491 | Anne de Bretagne marries Charles VIII of France |
| 1499 | Anne marries Louis XII of France |
| 1514 | Death of Anne de Bretagne |
| 1532 | Union of France and Brittany |
| 1589-98 | Wars of Religion |
| 1655 | New Parliament building at Rennes |
| 1675 | Revolt of the Bonnets Rouges |
| 1789 | French Revolution; Brittany divided into 5 depts. |
| 1791 | Counter-revolutionary movement (Chouans) |
| 1870 | Franco-Prussian war – Conlie incident |
| 1917 | American troops arrive in Brittany |
| 1921 | Brittany has France's first communist mayor |
| 1926 | Breton flag designed |
| 1940-44 | Germans occupy Brittany |
| 1941 | Loire Inférieure detached from Brittany |
| 1957 | Loire Inférieure becomes Loire Atlantique |
| 1978 | Wreck of Amoco Cadiz off Finistère |
| 1994 | Parliament Building at Rennes burnt down |

# 1 - MEN & STONES

Brittany is well known for its prolific prehistoric remains in the form of large stone structures (megaliths), but these were by no means the first signs of human life on the peninsula.

## Palaeolithic

The earliest known palaeolithic (early stone age) site in Brittany is at Saint-Malo-de-Phily where pieces of worked stone date human occupation of the area back to about 700,000BC. Further traces of activity from this period have been found at Menez Drégan on the Bay of Audierne, where cavemen lived around 450,000BC and knew the use of fire. At various sites, such as Mont-Dol, the bones and teeth of animals like mammoth, elephant and rhinoceros have been discovered.

## Mesolithic

As temperatures warmed and the sea-levels began to rise to usher in the Mesolithic period (about 10,000BC), hunter-gatherers left evidence of their existence in the form of skeletons and shell jewellery at burial sites on the Ile de Téviec off the Quiberon peninsula. Occupation of the interior also increased during this time - an atmospheric cave at Roc'h-Toul near Luzec was one of the first excavated sites, with hundreds of stone scrapers and cutters found. Flint tools were worked here from raw material brought from the area of the northern coast, where a seam of flint, at that time exposed, is now covered by the Channel.

## Neolithic

It is neolithic (new stone age) man, however, whose mark remains clearly imprinted on the country today. His world was a naked landscape of raw hills and dense forest: no buildings or towns, no masts or pylons, no roads or fences. The megalithic monuments he has left behind - standing stones, alignments and burial sites - should be looked at

Bay of Kernic

with this in mind, imagining the impact of the stone structures (and the many wooden ones which have not survived) when they were the only significant man-made features on view. Some today are half-submerged in estuary waters as sea-levels have continued to rise and are now about 10 metres higher.

Menhir de Kerloas

The period of this Neolithic civilisation in Brittany was approximately 5000-2000BC. Called 'prehistory' because it came before the age of written evidence, the surviving remains, both monuments and the artefacts found in or around them, allow archaeologists to provide a more detailed picture of this primitive people. Settling to a life on the land gave them more time to develop mental skills and resources, which doubtless contributed to the conception of their monuments. Accurate information about numbers and many other aspects of this era is impossible to gauge, but a reasonable estimate of the population of Brittany at this time would be about 100,000 people.

## Remains

Evidence of Neolithic man is widely spread throughout Brittany. Today these monuments are often collectively referred to as 'megaliths', whether or not they are built from the huge stones the name suggests. The most famous site is Carnac in Morbihan with its rows of over two thousand standing stones stretching for miles across the landscape. Just as impressive in their size and location are the lone menhirs like Kerloas in Finistère, the tallest one still standing in France at nearly 11m in height.

There are also many individual and collective burial sites where grave goods have been discovered. These do not necessarily reflect the date of construction of a monument, however, as the sacred sites continued to be used by later generations as places of burial and veneration. What we do know of the life and social organisation of Neolithic people in Brittany comes largely from the analysis of archaeological finds. To take a basic example, information about diet and lifestyle can be gleaned from the evidence of grains, pollen and animal bones found in burial chambers.

## Progress

The Neolithic era saw developing technology, with polished stone, pottery and weaving each making their appearance. More advanced than their nomadic hunter-gatherer forebears, the people of this time began to settle on the land, growing crops and raising livestock. From grain found stored in containers in burial chambers it is clear that barley (used to make beer as well as bread), wheat and millet were grown, whilst mill-stones and pestles for grinding the cereals have also been unearthed. Vegetables, herbs, berries and fruit were all available to supplement the basic diet, and flax was sometimes cultivated for use in garments and nets.

**Flint arrowhead**

Animals were also reared, with sheep, pigs and oxen providing milk, meat, skin and horns for sustenance and practical usage. Dogs were used for hunting, which, together with fishing, provided an important extra source of protein. Deer, boar and birds were available, to be tackled with bows and arrows or primitive spears.

Clearing of forested land for timber and settlement began in the interior of Brittany at this time. The small communities lived in simple huts, with timber frames and wattle and daub walls, within the protection of a fortified site. This would be surrounded by a defensive ditch and bank, reinforced by stake ring fences. Stone bases of huts remain at Le Lizo near Carnac, but these may be from the later Iron Age.

## Social Structure

Little is known about their social groupings, but the production of food over and above immediate needs, and storage of the surplus, certainly led to an increasing population. It is clear from the megalithic monuments that remain that large groups worked together on such projects, which required not only careful planning and execution, but also supplies which could provision the work-force. Several hundred people may have been needed to erect a standing stone, so a considerable amount of extra food would have been essential for the duration of this work.

Specialized skills, whether in managing supplies, directing operations or the building techniques involved, would have presumably commanded greater status than unskilled labour. All this suggests a hierarchical structure to their society to ensure the necessary organization and co-operation.

## Tools and Weapons

In this, the New Stone Age, stone was the main natural resource, fashioned and worked to provide essential tools and weapons. Flint was mostly imported as, apart from

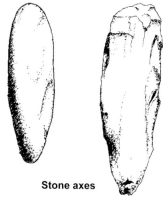

**Stone axes**

some coastal deposits, Brittany contains no natural sources of flint.

Cutting implements such as knives and polished stone axes for felling trees or tilling the soil have been found, as well as scrapers for use on animal skin or wood, and arrow-heads made from flint. Primitive picks were made from deer antlers. At Plussulien the same outcrop of

16

**Plussulien**

dolerite rock was used systematically for over 1,500 years for axe-making. Worked stone from this spot has been found as far afield as Aquitaine, Belgium and England. Unfinished stone was often exported to be finally shaped and polished elsewhere.

## Pottery

**Clay cooking pot**

Plain or simply decorated pottery was made from clay, although there were not the means to fire it at high temperatures and the quality of finds varies enormously. Cooking pots to hang over the fire were needed, rounded underneath at first, although later flat-bottomed vessels were produced. Because of the fragility of the pots, putting hot stones inside may have been a more reliable method of heating liquid. Simple containers and clay 'bottles' have also been found. In the late Neolithic period, wool was spun using pottery spindle weights.

## Religion

There has been wide speculation about the spiritual beliefs of this society and there is no definitive answer. It seems most likely that some kind of worship of the Sun and Moon and possibly other nature-based deities was at the core of their religious practices. The Tribunal at St-Just may have been an early calendar, with a marker stone positioned to read off the position of the setting or rising sun against a semi-circle of taller stones.

**Relief carving at Crec'h Quillé**

Phenomena such as thunder, lightning, flood or drought could bring destruction to the only resources a primitive agricultural society had for survival, so propitiation of the powers that caused these was vital. It was also just as natural to celebrate the benefits of fair weather, such as growth and harvest. A goddess of the earth and fertility may have been represented in stylised relief carving of pairs of breasts commonly found at burial sites (for example, at Crec'h Quillé near Perros-Guirec). Celebrations and feastings may also have accompanied the achievement of erecting the megaliths.

### Death and Burial
Clearly burial of the dead was a significant ritual for Neolithic man. Tombs of important figures were often aligned with the rising sun of the winter solstice, as at the Roche-aux-Fées, and, in the womb-like chambers, gifts for the journey to the after-life have been found – food, jewellery, weapons – relevant to the status of the deceased. Evidence of fires and pottery remnants found outside some tombs suggest that ancestors and the dead continued to be revered with rituals and ceremonies. Other rites of passage may have taken place in the vicinity of the tombs, in an age unawed by the close connection of life and death.

The earth in Brittany was generally not good at preserving bones (which needs limestone or alkaline soil) but finds include skeletons (sometimes scorched, as at La Torche), as well as weapons, jewellery, tools, utensils and food. Items of fabric, wood and leather have rotted away. There is an excellent museum of prehistory at Penmarc'h, where the results of many excavations of burial sites can be seen today.

## Dolmens

This name, dating from the 18th century, means stone (men) table (dol) in Breton. It does not signify the ritual sacrificial slab of popular imagination, but simply the basic structure of Neolithic burial chambers, with supporting uprights

**Near Menez Hom**

and one or more large capstones as a 'roof', placed by raising mounds of earth at the sides. Some buttressed graves, for example at Lesconil, probably never had covering slabs at all. Stones were transported to the chosen site using systems of rollers and pulleys: for the magnificent Roche-aux-Fées this involved a journey of more than 4 kilometres. Although originally earthed over, many dolmens have been opened up over the centuries by gradual erosion or for research or robbery, and only their exposed stone skeletons now remain. Many have lost stones which were taken away from the sites for other constructions.

**Roche-aux-Fées**

**Brennilis**

Dolmens in Brittany vary enormously in size and shape according to dates of construction, local conditions and original intentions. They began as simple passage graves, with an entrance leading to a single round or rectangular burial chamber. One of the oldest, dating from about 6000BC, is the tortoise-like Dolmen de Guilligui near Portsall. Other examples can be seen at the tomb of Kercado (c.4500BC) at Carnac or a smaller version at Brennilis, both still earth-covered. A later version, from about 3500BC, is apparent at the site of Mané Kerioned where the three dolmens widen towards the end in a wedge shape. One of these is underground and the vertical stones bear unusual carvings on their inner face.

**Mané Kerioned**

Another development was the gallery grave, a long rectangular chamber, sometimes divided internally by large slabs of stone, and with a similarly shaped covering mound originally. In Brittany a grave of this type is often called an allée couverte (covered alley), and numerous examples survive in varying states of preservation. The entrance may be found at the end or, as at Crec'h Quillé (c.2500BC), at right angles, a form also found at Tréal, near St-Just.

**Liscuis**

Some dolmens retain their original decoration in the form of relief carving which has symbolic as well as artistic significance. Axes, pairs of breasts and paddle or oar shaped objects are common motifs – all these figure at the impressive allée couverte at Mougou Bihan. The tomb of Kercado has an axe on the ceiling stone of its square chamber, whilst that on the island of Gavrinis is adorned by lavish swirls and snake-like forms.

The position and size of dolmens suggest that they were reserved for important figures, and collective burials would probably have been clan or family based. A low hill was a commonly chosen situation, possibly dominating the locality of a particular tribe. An interesting trio remains above the Gorges de Daoulas at Liscuis, but the marked concentrations of more elaborate graves lie around Carnac and Quiberon in Morbihan, and in Finistère around Penmarc'h.

## Cairns

Cairns are larger monuments with a series of burial chambers covered by a huge mound of smaller stones forming dry-stone walls. Most famous of these is the Cairn of Barnenez, in its exceptional location overlooking the Bay of Morlaix in Finistère. Other examples of cairns include one on the Ile de Gavrinis, the less well-known site of the Ile de Cairn near Ploudalmézeau and a well-preserved site at Dissignac, near St-Nazaire.

# THE CAIRN OF BARNENEZ

*The cairn was constructed over a period of hundreds of years from about 4500BC (according to radio-carbon dating), using dolerite building stone from 500m away and granite from a distance of about 2kms. There were two main phases of building, with the earliest section (to the east) comprising five burial chambers, each with a separate passage, and the later one six more. The cairn in total is 72m long, up to 25m wide and 8m high, containing the 11 dolmens, which have dry-stone walls and cap-stoned or domed roofs. The outside of the monument is stepped for stability and elongated to hug the terrain. Finds range from Neolithic polished axes and pottery to a later copper dagger and arrowhead. Symbolic designs on a few of the stones include axes, serpentine forms and an unusual 'goddess' head with spreading hair.*

*This extraordinary monument was properly discovered in the 1950s, when the site was used as a quarry for new road development and the first burial chamber was found. Subsequent wilful damage by the developer was the subject of a successful prose-cution, and, once the site was classified as of major historical importance, excavations were carried out at Barnenez, near Morlaix, between 1955 and 1968. Careful restoration work followed.*

## Menhirs

Menhirs ('long stone' in Breton) or standing-stones, although not unique to Brittany, are found more commonly here than elsewhere in Europe. They range in height from little over a metre to almost 11m high. The type of stone depended on what was available fairly locally, as transport over long distances was difficult. Wood was also needed for moving the huge stones, where rollers were the most likely method for movement over fairly flat terrain. It is thought that some were transported by water, strapped beneath rafts constructed around them.

Granite was the best material and, if extracted from a typical gorge chaos (where huge granite boulders, split by fissures, are piled on top of each other) was often pre-shaped. Examples of impressive shaped stones can be seen at Champ Dolent and Kergadiou. Schist and quartz were also used in smaller menhirs. The stones were raised by banking and the leverage of wooden poles, with ropes made from natural plant fibres. Once in place, the holes were filled with small stones – flint and shards of pottery are sometimes found in this position – and earth. In some places (St-Just, for example) fire-pits at the foot of a menhir may be an indication of ceremonial activity.

Many have disappeared, been broken, used for building stone or moved from their original location. The enormous stone at Locmariaquer is now fallen and broken, but it would have measured an astonishing 20m and weighed

**St-Just**

about 300 tons. Of those surviving, all have been eroded by the elements to some extent, which has destroyed or made almost indecipherable much artistic decoration. Patterns and representational designs were carved in relief or incised in the stone. Snakes embellish the menhir of Le Manio at Carnac, and animals and axes, barely visible now, decorate the leaning stone at St-Samson-sur-Rance.

The stone circles familiar from Britain are rare in Brittany. The standing stones were sometimes part of alignments (in rows), sometimes with other stones and sometimes singular. There may well have been some connection in the placing of lone stones, even those a considerable distance apart, and many mark the site of burial chambers. They were sited in various positions in the landscape, often on hillsides (rather than hill-tops), by the coast, or near springs, such as those at Goasker near Callac. Impressive alignments, apart from the extraordinary profusion at Carnac, can be seen at Camaret and St-Just.

Nobody knows exactly what the menhirs were for, and postulations range from the mundane to the fanciful. Landmarks, 'signposts', boundary markers, statements of power, focus for fertility rituals, calendars fixing the solstices, sightlines for astrological and astronomical calculations are favourite suppositions, and modern studies continue to investigate the connections between the numerous separate stones (possibly placed in a visible chain over large distances) and the alignments.

## New Horizons and the Bronze Age

The erection of the megaliths continued into what is now called the Bronze Age (approx.2000-1000BC). New influences were being felt in Brittany, with the use of metals: first copper – introduced perhaps by incomers from the Iberian peninsula – and then the tougher alloy of bronze, achieved by the inclusion of tin, which was at first imported from Cornwall but later mined locally at, for example, St-Renan and Penestin.

Round burial tumuli became increasingly common in the interior of the Armorican peninsula as occupation spread. These, devoted to single burials, suggest a shift in importance from collective identity to that of individuals, some of whom were clearly wealthy in possessions. Before the first proper excavation of that at Tanouédou near

**Tumulus de Tanouédou**

Bourbriac in the 19th century, the owner of the land was killed by falling debris as he dug in search of buried treasure. The tumulus is 40m in diameter and yielded finds of a bronze axe, swords and gold jewellery.

In the later Bronze Age some axe-heads of the socketed type (haches à douille) were manifestly unsuitable for practical use due to their flimsy design and high lead content. These were probably used as a form of monetary exchange or votive offering: a cache of more than 900 was found at Plurien, for example.

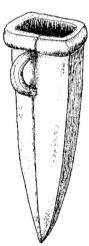

Widespread trading contacts established in the Neolithic period, with both raw materials and products such as polished axes from Brittany being found as far afield as Holland, southern England and the Rhône valley, were developed in the Bronze Age. Jewellery in the form of beads and necklaces was imported, with identified sources including the Alpine regions. It is clear that there was much travel by sea and contact with other lands long before the arrival of the Celts.

**Hache à douille (socketed axe)**

# 2 - CELTS & ROMANS

The origin of the Celts has been the subject of much recent debate, with arguments mainly against racial unity and in favour of cultural affinities between the many different tribes that spread across Europe from the area between Russia and the Black Sea after about 700BC.

This was a gradual process over hundreds of years, and, as far as the Amorican peninsula is concerned, it is impossible to say with certainty to what extent they conquered or rather slowly infiltrated the north western corner of France. Those that settled in the region of modern France became known as the Gauls.

These Celts had iron weapons, which were superior to those made of bronze, and made use of cavalry in warfare. They brought their own languages, culture and religion to the area of modern Brittany, which was part of what they called Are Mori (land bordering the sea). Visual evidence today, apart from museum exhibits, is mainly confined to hill-fort defences and the numerous archaeological digs which continue to yield artefacts and new information. Stone built remains date mainly from the later period known as Gallo-Romano, after the Roman invasion in the 1st century BC.

Written evidence begins during this period, although not from the Celts themselves, whose traditions were oral. Greek and Roman writers attest the presence of Celtic peoples in western Europe at this time: Pytheas, for example, during his voyage around the coast of Brittany in about 320BC, records the Osismes as a group already established there.

## Tribes and states

The structure of this Celtic society was tribal, and by the 2nd century BC there were five such states in Brittany: the Osismes in Finistère and part of what is now Côtes d'Armor, the Coriosolites to the east with the Riedones beyond, the Namnètes around the Loire and the Vénètes, roughly in the

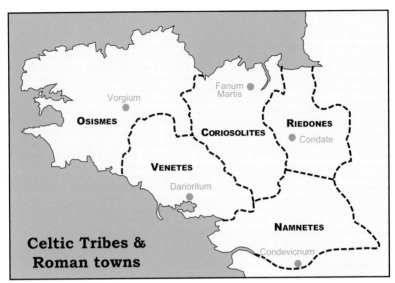

**Celtic Tribes & Roman towns**

area of Morbihan (see map). According to Julius Caesar, the latter were the most powerful by virtue of their fine ships, in which they were accustomed to sail to Britain. Each

**Coin of the Riedones**

state was independent, minting their own coinage, pursuing their own trading links and involved in a shifting pattern of alliances and aggressions with their neighbours. For the great majority of the Gallic Celts, life was still essentially a rural one.

## Social and political structure

The tribes were divided into large family-based clans, and society was hierarchical, with warrior nobles commanding the greatest prestige, then those of special status such as the Druids and skilled craftsmen, followed by free men and finally slaves, who were debtors or war captives. The role of women has also been the subject of much research, as they played a strong and active part in Celtic society.

Whilst these Gallic tribes might be prepared to follow a single leader for a limited time in war, they generally maintained a strong sense of independence. In fact, they were inclined to quarrel, and inter-tribal warfare, in which any available allies would be used against enemies, was common. Their lack of unity, despite great bravery on the battlefield, was a major factor in the Roman acquisition of Gaul.

## Settlements
They lived in round or rectangular huts of wattle-and-daub with thatched roofs, some as great as 20m in length, with the hearth being the main feature of the interior. Stone bases for this type of house, dating from about 1000BC, have been excavated. Outbuildings and stables were needed for storage and animals, and examples of storage vaults have also been discovered, where a well-shaft and passage lead to several underground rooms. They grew mainly cereal crops, now helped by the use of iron ploughshares in tilling the soil. Pigs, sheep, cows and horses were kept, the latter usually for war.

As with earlier settlements, some of which were taken over by these newcomers, a palisade and bank or ditch provided an outer defence. Remains of an Iron Age enclosure and later Gallo-Romano settlement can be seen at Kersigneau-Saint-Jean, near Audierne, and there are many hill-forts from this period, including, for example, one in the forest at Huelgoat. At Alet, on the right bank of the Rance, a fortified spur protected the entrance to the port, an important source of cross channel trade long before the development of St-Malo.

## Crafts and trade
The Celts are renowned for the fine quality of their craftsmanship. In addition to iron tools and weapons, they made superb leather, wood and metalwork. Exceptional pieces include a gold platter showing Hercules and Bacchus found in Rennes in 1774 and a gold collar discovered near Brest in 1985. Pottery was now elaborately decorated, often with geometric patterns of inter-connecting spirals. They also wove wool and linen, using natural dyes to colour the cloth.

The peninsula had strong links with Britain and other parts of Europe. The earliest contacts with the mighty Roman empire were economic ones, in addition to trade with the rest of Gaul across the Loire, and also Ireland and

Spain. Commerce was well-developed, with the export of pottery, pewter and salt. Widespread importation of Italian wine is witnessed by many finds of amphorae (pottery wine containers). Tin from Cornwall came into Corbilo and then some went on further afield, as Brittany was a staging post in Britain's links with the Mediterranean area.

## Religion

The Druids, who combined the roles of priests, judges and bards, were a unifying and highly influential factor in Celtic society. Their name may derive from the oak (derw) and mean oak wisdom or great wisdom (dru+iudd), and their tradition was an oral one, with the responsibility to preserve knowledge and practice to be passed on through the generations. They also held the secrets of prophecy and divination, power tools in an age of uncertainty.

Celtic religion was polytheistic, with the spirit of divinity attributed to all living things, and places such as groves of trees, springs and hill-tops like Menez Hom and Menez Bré held sacred. Male and female deities were worshipped, such as Lug(h), a god associated by Julius Caesar with the Roman god Mars. Statuettes of Epona, a goddess usually connected with horses, have been discovered at various places such as Nantes and Quimper.

Many votive offerings have emerged from excavations and many stone stele survive – an interesting one at Bécherel has a male figure (possibly a god associated with fertility) on one side and three animal heads on the other.

The Celts seem to have believed in the immortality of the soul and reincarnation, so grave goods were significant, with food, jewellery and weapons necessary for the journey of the dead and their next life. Both burial and cremation, attested by funerary urns, were practised.

**Stele at Bechérel**

## The arrival of the Romans

The ambition of Julius Caesar, who as pro-consul built an armed power-base in Gaul (very roughly France), led to the expansion of Roman power throughout that territory, eventually including the north-west.

In 56BC, after Roman failure to defeat the Vénètes decisively on land, Caesar's response was to have a fleet built on the Loire. At sea he was victorious, achieving one of the few great Roman naval successes. Securing the coastline was strategically important: in the following year, Caesar was to make his first (relatively unsuccessful) expedition to Britain. In 52BC the Coriosolites, Riedones and Osismes all sent forces to try to relieve the siege of Alesia, in Burgundy, where Vercingetorix was in difficulties. Failure to achieve this, and the Gallic chief's subsequent surrender signalled the futility of resistance to Roman rule in Gaul.

The Celtic land of Ar-mor(ic) became the Roman territory of Armorica, part of the province of Gallia Lugdunensis, which had a distant capital at Lyons. This did not mean, however, a sudden flooding of the territory with a toga-wearing, Latin speaking population. Roman troops and officials were certainly in evidence, but Celtic nobles, increasingly Romanised, would have played the most active part in local administration and thousands of rural dwellers probably saw only gradual change to their lives in the Gallo-Romano period of the first three centuries AD.

## Towns and communications

The Romans organized the area with their usual administrative zeal. Each tribe's territory (civitas) had a main town which provided the political, religious and commercial centre for the area, such as Fanum Martis (shrine of Mars, now Corseul) for the Coriosolites and Vorgium (Carhaix) for the Osismes. The surrounding countryside was further divided into smaller districts. A deliberative assembly met regularly and saw to the smooth running of administrative and financial systems. Inscriptions from this period from Rennes, for example, mention the Senate of the Riedones and magistrates (the Roman term for executive officials), who would have been drawn from the local aristocracy.

The effects of Roman civilisation were felt most keenly in

Corseul

an urban context. Some existing towns like Condate (Rennes) and Condevicnum (Nantes) were taken over and expanded, whilst others such as Darioritum (Vannes) and Vorgium (Carhaix) were created, laid out along traditional Roman principles with a central forum and grid plan lay-out of streets. At Corseul today the remains of a Roman street can still be seen.

Communications, essential for the military, were also improved by a network of well-built Roman roads for the swift transport of men and supplies. Two major routes passed through Rennes: the first to Corseul, Morlaix, Kerilien and Pointe-St-Mathieu on the Atlantic coast, and the second via Loudéac to Carhaix and then to the Aber Wrac'h. Another important road (from Bordeaux) passed through Nantes, Vannes and Quimper to the Pointe du Raz. Remains of Gallo-Romano bridges can be seen on a grand scale at Pont Crac'h on the Aber Wrac'h and a much smaller, well-preserved one at Callac.

Ports were well-organised, with large-scale transport of goods across the channel possible. Finds from a wreck off Ploumanac'h include a sizeable cargo of 24 tons of lead ingots.

## Roman civilisation

Even in this far flung region of the Empire, a settled period of Roman administration fostered economic development in trade, the exploitation of the land and its resources, and the skills of its craftsmen. The Romans established or took over mines for lead/silver (Poullaouen), gold (Besné), iron (Quintin) and tin (Saint-Renan).

Offering the benefits of Roman civilization was another way

of encouraging harmony and stability with the local population. Archaeology has revealed that there were public baths at Corseul, for example, and a theatre at Kerilien, near Lesneven. Remains of a remarkable aqueduct can still be seen at Carhaix-Plouguer (see p.34). Basilicas (covered law-courts and meeting places) were built at Rennes and Vannes.

**Temple of Mars, Corseul**

In accordance with their customary expedient practice, the Romans encouraged the association of local gods with their own deities. A bronze statuette of Minerva found at Dinéault also bears on the helmet a swan symbol more commonly associated with Celtic goddesses. The most remarkable Roman religious building to survive, however, is an octagonally shaped temple to Mars near Corseul.

The earliest arrival of Christianity also came with the Romans, and by the time that they gave up control of the region it is clear that churches were already well-established in the eastern part of Brittany. These followed the tradition of Rome, with Latin as the language of liturgy and of record-keeping. In an early trial of faith, Donatien and Rogatien, two brothers from Nantes, who refused to renounce their faith at the time of Christian persecution by the Roman Emperor Diocletian, were tortured and executed at the end of the 3rd century. A bishop (probably not the first) of Rennes, named Athenius, is known to have attended the Council of Tours in 461.

More than 5,000 rural sites of small villas and farmhouses from this period have been discovered in Brittany, often by chance. An archaeological dig of a medieval settlement near La Feuillée, for example, has turned up some foundations from the Roman period.

Near Roche-Maurice, a villa dating to AD60-80, covered a large area. The house itself was 25m long, with a colonnade,

**Bath house, Hogolo**

kitchen, various living rooms and bedrooms and a small bath-house. Another excavated in the 1980s at Châtillon-sur-Seiche was essentially a farm complex with baths and a hypocaust (under-floor) heating system. A compact bath-house suite at Hogolo on the coast of Côtes d'Armor would have served a country house nearby.

Some knowledge of individuals in this period can be gleaned from the discovery of Latin inscriptions, such as those dedicating offerings to the gods, or epitaphs. For example, a poignant vignette emerges of Silicia Namgidde, of African origin, who followed her son to Corseul. He honoured her exceptional devotion in an epitaph there on her death at the age of 65.

An unusual and particularly interesting site is the Roman garum factory in the Plomarc'h on the edge of Douarnenez. Here in a magnificent setting overlooking the sea, a pungent sauce made from rotting fish-entrails was produced in very large quantities to satisfy the demand for this essential food seasoning. At Resto, near Lanester in Morbihan, there is another example of a small seasoning enterprise with four stone tanks.

**Garum factory, Plomarc'h.**

# CARHAIX

*This town was the capital of the Osismes, and evidence for its Roman name of Vorgium comes from a military mile-post discovered near Maël-Carhaix. It was founded early in the 1st century AD at the nerve centre of its civitas, an important focal point for communications in the west. Vorgium was built on traditional Roman principles with two main streets crossing at the centre (rues Lancien and Briseux - the latter meaning cobbled street) and a grid plan for the surroundings. The town covered c150 hectares, with cemeteries to the east and west. The size of the settlement, its facilities and the quality of some of the foundations attest the status of Vorgium, although no public buildings have yet been discovered. Many artefacts, including coins, jewellery, pottery and glass funerary urns have been found.*

*Excavations during work on the hospital site in 1995 revealed foundations of a large villa complex, with four wings around a central garden. Many rooms, including living rooms with underfloor heating (by the hypocaust system) were found. Examination of a nearby area has revealed a section of the Roman town including streets lined by shops, workshops or taverns, backed by private houses with peristylia (interior courtyard gardens) and their own bath-houses.*

*The 3rd century aqueduct brought water from 27kms away. It followed the contours of the land (with the exception of one long tunnel) through Paule, Glomel and*  *Persivien, to maintain a natural fall for the water to reach the town. It was mainly a subterranean canal, covered by slabs of slate, but a bridge of 900m was necessary for the last stage to cross a dip and bring water to the town centre. From collection in a water tower, it was then dispersed to public fountains and*

**Aqueduct**

*baths through a series of pipes. There was also an allied drainage and sewage disposal system.*

*In the Place de la Tour d'Auvergne, a late 3rd century coin hoard was found, indicating the increasingly precarious state of affairs for Vorgium's inhabitants. During the 4th century the site was gradually abandoned, with the political seat of the civitas moving to Brest, a better defensive position.*

## End of Roman rule

By the end of the 3rd century AD, the cohesion of the Roman Empire was weakening, under threat from many new invaders. Eginhart's 9th century history of Gaul claims that Britons fleeing the Saxons took over territory from the Coriosolites at this time.

Gaul was attacked by the Franks, whilst Pictish, Saxon and Friesian pirates took advantage of the growing mayhem to pillage the coastal areas. Economic and social disruption were rife. Indications of this troubled time include fortification works undertaken, for example at Brest, St-Brieuc and Vannes, and the preference of Alet to Corseul as a defensive base for the Coriosolites, where the Roman military headquarters used around the 370s has been discovered. Later discovery of many buried coin hoards, never reclaimed by the owners who abandoned properties in fear of their lives, are another sign of general upheaval. (It should also be said, however, that some archaeologists regard these rather as ritual offerings.) At Landébaeron, near Guingamp, a trove of more than 5,000 coins was found, and over 16,000 in a single hoard near Rennes. A fine example can be seen in the Musée des Beaux Arts at Vannes.

The general Maximus, in command of Roman forces in Britain, withdrew to the continent in a bid for supreme power in about AD383. He brought with him British troops, perhaps with a view to defending the northern coasts from increasingly frequent raids by pirates. The monk Gildas' lurid account describes Britain's loss of many young men ('ingenti iuventute spoliata') who never returned, and many of these may have remained to settle across the channel in Armorica. Maximus himself moved on southwards, only to be defeated and executed by his rivals in Italy.

Further attempts were made to bolster the coastal defences, but essentially direct Roman power in Brittany was over. On the one hand this period had seen material benefits for the region, but on the other it had planted the seeds of future division between written Latin culture and the oral tradition of local languages. There was also a marked contrast between the Roman church in the east and the entrenched paganism of the ruder west, although the latter was soon to receive fresh input to its religious development.

# 3 - DEPARTURE & ARRIVALS

The period after the departure of the Roman military and administration is often called the Dark Ages, a confusing time when contemporary records are rare and history may be barely distinguishable from legend. Although written accounts become increasingly frequent from the 6th century onwards, the accuracy and reliability of each is still a subject of debate. For example, the dynasties of Frankish kings (Merovingians and then Carolingians) in control of neighbouring France generated record-keeping which provides evidence for the later part of this period, and Gregory, Bishop of Tours in the 6th century, wrote a History of the Franks, with many (usually derogatory) references to Brittany. These works were in Latin, the customary language of church scholarship and the Frankish court at this time.

Certainly the Armorican peninsula felt the force of barbarian raids, as archaeological evidence of the burning of buildings shows. Many inhabitants may have fled their homes or lost their lives, but it is impossible to know the full extent of the disruption and depopulation. Similarly, political institutions, such as they were in the early part of this period, are undocumented. The area fragmented into the hands of various individuals who built up their own power bases.

Geoffrey of Monmouth, who wrote a history of the kings of Britain more than 600 years later, says that before his ill-fated Italian campaign Maximus 'bequeathed' royal power in Armorica to a Briton, Conan Meriadec. From Conan, some say, sprang a line of early Breton 'kings' such as the legendary Gradlon. It seems strange that no other sources mentioned Conan in the intervening centuries, and many scholars today do not credit his existence as a distinct historical entity, but rather a semi-literary creation to please Geoffrey's patron, Henry I (who would relish a British line with royal power in France). Conan remains, however, a bright figure in popular thought much in the way of another Dark Age legend, King Arthur.

## Legends

King Arthur (although the familiar stories about him are medieval) also has his hold on Brittany with the Forest of Paimpont identified with the magical forest Broceliande, where Merlin fell in love with Viviane, who trapped false lovers in the Valley of No Return. The château of Comper is said to have been her palace. Merlin's 'tomb' is situated in the forest near the Fountain of Barenton, the waters of which conferred eternal youth. In Finistère, sites in the forest at Huelgoat bear the name of Arthur's Grotto and Arthur's camp, although archaeology has shown the latter to be originally an Iron Age hill-fort, with various later use, including a medieval motte.

Evidence for much of the early part of this period is a mixture of history and legend: witness the story of King Gradlon and Ys, the Breton Atlantis, a city drowned by the sea for the wickedness of princess Dahut after the warnings of St-Corentin were ignored. It is said the church bells of Ys can still be heard echoing beneath the waves of the Bay of Douarnenez. Archaeological evidence suggests that at least some buildings were covered by the sea here. At low tide, remains of walls can be seen under the water below the Plomarc'h and at the Pointe du Ry. Gradlon, traditionally the king of Quimper, is also said to have granted St-Guenolé the land on which he founded the famous abbey at Landévennec in its exceptional setting at the mouth of the Aulne (see page 56).

## New arrivals

What is certain is that this was a time of change and new directions, as immigrants from Britain came to join the existing population of Gallo-Romano Armorica. The earliest of the Britons, as mentioned in the previous chapter, came during the 3rd century to bolster the Roman coastal defences of Armorica against the increasing number and strength of barbarian raids.

From the 4th century onwards, small groups of immigrants of mainly Celtic origin, from Cornwall, Wales and Ireland, began to cross the channel to settle in the land that came to be called 'little Britain' or Brittany, in place of

Amorica. (Some also settled further east around the Seine estuary and others in north-western Spain.) To what extent this movement was a specific response to the inroads of Anglo-Saxon invasions across the Channel is uncertain: there was no mass exodus, but essentially a gradual and peaceful process over hundreds of years. Although they cannot all have been hospitably welcomed, there is no suggestion of concerted opposition to this incoming population. Trading links and contact between these peoples had been firmly established for centuries – the crossing of the channel was only a day's journey – and there were close linguistic affinities. The Breton language in its various dialects, derived from the similar Celtic languages of Dark Age immigrants and the existing population, began to develop at this time.

Often the in-comers were organised groups of men, women and children, including religious leaders, who were prepared to negotiate for and purchase land to settle on. Those of the tribe of the Dumnonii from Cornwall settled in the north of Brittany (which came to be called Domnonée) and the Cornovii from north Wales in the south west (Cornouaille), gradually taking over and replacing the old tribal areas.

Three main territories now covered the region up to the Vilaine river (see map), with two of these reflecting the new

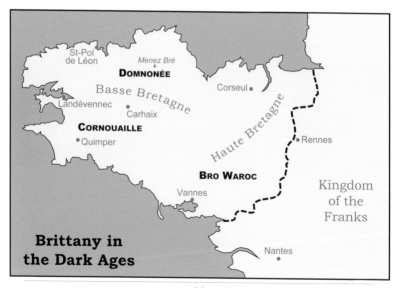

Brittany in the Dark Ages

immigrations and subsequent settlements that characterised this time. There was a clear difference of development between the west of the region (Basse Bretagne) and the more Romanised east (Haute Bretagne), which also inevitably came into closer contact with the kingdom of the Franks. From the reign of Clovis in the late 5th century AD this extended over much of modern France.

## Christianity in the west

From the 5th century onwards, the spread of Christianity in the west of Brittany became rapid and widespread. Many monks were among the new arrivals here, and they lost little time in attempting to convert their new land. Among these were to be some of the earliest Breton saints – Pol, Tugdual, Samson, Malo and Brieuc. St-Pol arrived with a handful of followers, St-Brieuc landed at the Aber Wrac'h with 168 people. Legend said that some came in 'stone boats': the remains of St-Conogan's petrified craft, for example, (actually a fallen menhir), can be seen by the Moulin de Keriolet on Cap Sizun. These simple men mostly followed the strict rule of St-Columba and sought to establish monasteries with their followers. In the 17th century, Albert Le Grand of Morlaix wrote his influential 'Lives of the Breton Saints', which became a seminal religious text, alongside the bible, and fostered the cults of these religious leaders.

The traditional seven founders of Christianity here were later honoured by Bretons, probably from the 12th century, in the Tro Breizh – a pilgrimage of over 700kms to visit the cathedrals at St-Pol-de-Léon, Tréguier (St-Tugdual), Dol (St-Samson), St-Malo, St-Brieuc, Vannes (St-Patern) and Quimper (St-Corentin).

Many of the Breton saints were healers, their names now connected with fountains on the sites of springs, places formerly associated with pagan worship. The blind Saint Hervé, who was led by a wolf, created the curative spring on Menez Bré, where a chapel in his honour still stands.

**Chapel of St-Hervé, Menez Bré**

He also founded a monastery at Lanrivoaré, and his hermitage remains in woodland nearby.

St-Hervé's hermitage

The existing religion the monks found in this western area was a mixture of Graeco-Roman and Celtic, with folk-lore and magic deep-rooted among the general population. The influence of the Druids was still strong, honouring the spirits and life-force of nature in trees and springs, for example. The early pioneers of Christianity in this region had an on-going struggle with established polytheistic paganism – hence the symbolic stories of saints who overcame monsters and performed miracles which aped the powers of older deities, the building of chapels on pagan sacred sites such as hill-tops and the later custom of carving crosses into the top of menhirs, those all too phallic reminders of their earthier predecessors. Paganism was to survive this onslaught through the oral traditions of poetry and song which continued to transmit the legends of popular belief down the generations.

From this period originate many of the distinctive Breton place-names still in evidence today. The prefix 'plou', meaning parish (e.g. Ploudaniel, Plougastel), reflects the earliest settlements of the immigrants and 'lan' (holy place) their religious establishments (Lampaul, Landivisiau). The concentration of names of this type along the coast, particularly in northern Finistère and Cornouaille, indicates the areas of most intensive new settlement during these centuries.

Men Marz, near Brignogan Plage

## St-Pol (St Paul Aurélien)

St-Pol came to Brittany from Wales with twelve companions in the early 5th century AD. Landing first on the island of Ouessant, he built a chapel and houses there where the town of Lampaul now stands. He then crossed to the northern coast and, via Lampaul-Ploudalmezeau, made his way to the castle of Léon. On the way, according to legend, he crossed the Aber Wrac'h by the Pont Crac'h (Devil's Bridge), one of the oldest bridges in Brittany. A small chapel dedicated to Pol Prat (St-Pol) is today nearby.

He was given land, including the Ile de Batz, by Count Withur, and established a monastery on the island and another at what is now St-Pol-de-Léon. He was a reluctant establishment figure and, despite becoming bishop under pressure, preferred a contemplative life on Batz, where he died in old age.

On the island today (a short boat trip from Roscoff harbour) the church preserves the stole which, according to legend, St-Pol used like a lead to subdue and drive out the terrifying local dragon, which then hurled itself over the cliff at Toull ar Sarpant (serpent's hole) on the north-western coast. This story is a typical example of the Christian symbolism for rooting out paganism.

In addition to the cathedral church of St-Pol-de-Léon, where  the Celtic bell given to him by Withur (or by a fish in another legend) can be seen, other churches are dedicated to him – Lampaul-Plouarzel, Lampaul (Ouessant) and Lampaul-Guimiliau, for example, as the names indicate. At the latter there is a fine 17th century banner honouring the saint. A life of St-Pol was written in 884 by Wrmonoc, a monk at Landévennec Abbey.

## Christianity in the East

In the south and east of Brittany, Christianity, brought by the Romans, was already well-established in the main towns, but here the Church of Rome rather than the Celtic church held sway. In the 5th century there were bishops, under the Pope's auspices, in Rennes and Nantes. St-Patern became the first bishop of Vannes around 460. A great cathedral at Nantes was built by Bishop Felix and the 6th century Melaine, Bishop of Rennes, was famous for his piety. St-Gildas founded a monastery at Rhuys.

The church here, in contrast to western Brittany, was a more urban organisation, with rituals from the Roman church, and worldly clergy far removed from the Breton monks of Basse Bretagne who often sought a life of prayer and solitude. A 6th century joint letter from three bishops to two Breton priests survives – an expression of disquiet that their simple brethren were allowing women to participate in the celebration and administration of mass, a practice natural to Celtic society, where women had a strong role, but abhorred by the Roman church.

## Society

Society at this time was still tribal, comprising extended family units, and legendary early 'kings' were basically tribal chieftains who dominated their locality. They and the nobility who supported them in warfare were maintained by the work of peasants on the land: these in fact could still be bought and sold with the property. There were also enslaved prisoners of war to swell the workforce.

A new development in this period was the establishment of 'machtierns,' officials mainly concerned with judicial and administrative affairs, often mentioned in abbey records. They lived in fortified residences or courts called 'les' or 'lis' (as survives in the name of Lesneven, for example, and many hamlets). At Carentoir in Morbihan, Jarnithin is attested as one of the earliest named machtierns and he was succeeded by his son and then grandson. Women could also apparently hold this office, as Aourken did at Carentoir, and they could also buy, sell and own property in their own right.

## Conomor

In the 6th century, pieces of the historical jigsaw become more numerous. There is much fragmentary evidence for the existence of Conomor (c.540), a chief originally from Cornwall now established in Brittany, who was later given the epithet 'Bluebeard.' Stories connect him with the Forest of Carnoët, and the Forest of Quénécan, south of Lac Guerlédan, as well as Carhaix, his original power-base, which may have got its name from his former residence in Cornwall at Carhays. From here as Comte de Poher, he controlled roughly the old territory of the Osismes. There is evidence for his other strategic bases at Gouesnou and Castel-Beuzit-Lanmeur, and at Montafilant near Corseul after an important extension of his power into the kingdom of Domnonée by marrying the widow of the last ruler, who died fortuitously.

Conomor is mentioned by Gregory of Tours as a Breton count and in some much later records of saints' lives as a prefect of the king of France. In this latter case, he may have had a brief to oversee maritime affairs between Britain and Brittany and the defence of the coast against barbarian

## GREGORY OF TOURS (c.539-594)

*The future Bishop of Tours was born to wealthy Gallo-Roman parents in the main town of the Auvergne region. His family was of distinguished descent, related to Saint Gregory, Bishop of Langres, and many of his relations were of high rank in the Church. Gregory himself was later to describe how his own brother Peter was murdered in Langres by the son of a man he was accused of killing by 'magic arts' as a potential rival for office. This incident gives something of the flavour of Gregory's most famous work, The History of the Franks, which tells of the cruel and violent times of the early Merovingian kings. He was altogether a prolific writer (in his native Latin language) mainly on religious themes such as Miracles, Lives of the Fathers and the Offices of the Church.*

*Gregory became Bishop of Tours in 573, and as such had authority over other sees, including those of Nantes and Rennes, then in the territory of the Franks. He describes how Bretons attacked these cities repeatedly, taking many of the inhabitants captive, burning and pillaging. He also gives an account of Waroc's raid in 587, when the Breton leader seized the vineyards around Nantes, harvested the grapes and took the wine produced with him back to Vannes.*

raids. He was certainly a capable, ambitious, bellicose chief, with energetic determination to enlarge his sphere of control.

In legend, Conomor, a sadistically cruel man, was supposed to have murdered many members of his family,

 most famously his young second wife Triphine, daughter of the Count of Vannes. He cut off the head of this unfortunate girl when she became pregnant, because of a prophecy that he would be killed by his own son. St-Gildas performed a miracle to restore her body to life, although Conomor still succeeded in beheading her infant son, Trémeur, years later.

So terrible was Conomor's reputation that a council of nobles and religious leaders was convoked on the summit of Menez Bré (near Guingamp), which resulted in his excommunication and he became an outcast in his own kingdom, despite connections at the court of the Frankish king

St-Trémeur

Childebert. St-Samson, bishop of Dol, finally persuaded Childebert of the justice of Conomor's exile from the church and persuaded him to release Judual, Conomor's stepson, who was being held, a 'guest' without freedom of movement, at the court.

Conomor was finally defeated in battle near Le Relecq in the Monts d'Arrée by Judual, but it was a savage, bloody contest. A sepulchre for the remains of victims of this struggle gave the place, later famous for its abbey, the name of Relecq (= reliques).

Even if stories of his extreme cruelty have a kernel of truth, Conomor's dynamic ambition and compelling urge to expand his territory seem characteristic of his age and a signifier of what was to follow in the next centuries as Breton leaders gained in political confidence.

**Excommunication of Conomor**
**(Church at Pedernec)**

## Brittany and the Franks

Although Frankish interest in Brittany began as early as the 5th century, relations between Brittany and the kings of the Merovingian dynasty had been relatively amicable during the reigns of Clovis and then his son Childebert. It is possible that successful Breton resistance to early attempts at domination led to a peace known to have been signed with

Clovis at the end of the 5th century, after his conversion to Christianity. This latter event was an important factor in amicable relations between the two peoples, and the treaty may have been encouraged by the bishops of Rennes and Vannes. Clovis acknowledged the territories of the Amorican tribes, and they, in turn, acknowledged the supremacy of the Franks, now rapidly expanding their empire across France.

There is no clear evidence of tribute paid by the Bretons to the Franks as a matter of course. Procopius, a Greek historian writing in the 6th century, describes the men who dwelt on the coast facing Britain as fishermen, farmers and traders, subject to the Franks, but without tribute. There is, however, some confusion in his account of Britain (and Brittany), as his information was derived only from contact with Franks who travelled on an embassy to the Byzantine court at Constantinople in 553.

Certain Breton chiefs (such as Conomor) seem to have been on good terms with the court at Paris, perhaps installed or at least supported by the Merovingian kings in return for supervision of affairs in Brittany, as the centre of Frankish control was too far removed for close personal attention to events in the far west.

Things changed after the death of Childebert in 558: power struggles within the Frankish court weakened and distracted the potential opponents of the Bretons, who were not slow to take advantage. The territories of Rennes and Vannes, areas which were always defensive military ones, looking east rather than west, became increasingly the object of border struggles between Bretons and Franks. The line of the Vilaine and Couesnon rivers was a rough boundary of Breton autonomy as political development in this period saw the start of an on-going struggle between Brittany and the kings of what became France.

The south eastern region of Brittany at this time came to be called Bro-waroc (the territory of Waroc) or Broérec. Waroc, a chieftain from the area of Vannes, fought the Franks assiduously, pushing eastwards in raids towards the end of the 6th century. He adopted the remarkably successful tactic of making treaties and giving undertakings when it was expedient to do so, and then renewing the armed struggle at the first opportunity.

At the beginning of the 7th century, Judicaël, chief of

Domnonée, also began to assert himself against the Franks and was successful in three battles (according to Pierre Le Baud who wrote in the 15th century) before making a treaty with the Frankish king Dagobert in 638. Judicaël later retired from a position of political power to enter a monastery. For his achievements and the moral tenure of his life, he was later regarded as a saint by the Bretons (the title 'saint' at this time denoting a respected religious leader, not someone canonised by the Catholic church).

## The Carolingians

Pepin the Short became King of the Franks in 752, the first famous member of the new Carolingian dynasty. He determined to reassert his authority in Brittany and soon took control of Vannes. He also established a border zone or 'Marche de Bretagne' and possibly appointed Frankish Prefects or Counts of the Marches to maintain order in this area, which was a buffer-zone between Brittany and the territories of Le Mans and Angers.

Roland, subject of the famous Song of Roland (a heroic poem about his death at the Battle of Roncevaux in 778, which was widely sung by troubadours of the Middle Ages), was described as Prefect of the Marches of Brittany. He may also have been the nephew of Charlemagne, Pepin's successor, indicating the importance placed on an appointment in this defensive area.

Certainly from this point the history of Brittany is dominated by the endless see-sawing of aggression and defence, gains and losses on both sides, and the consequent misery for inhabitants of the borderlands that were so keenly fought over by both Bretons and Franks (later French).

In 799, the Annals of the Frankish Kings claimed that Brittany was entirely under the control of Charlemagne who was crowned Holy Roman Emperor the following year. As soon became clear, this was very far from being the case.

# 4 · KINGS & VIKINGS

The great Charlemagne himself soon found further incursions necessary. In 811 he was in the area of St-Malo, where even churches and monasteries were destroyed during the campaign. His son Louis the Pious succeeded him in 814 and faced continued revolts led by fiery figureheads.

## Morvan

The Breton leader Morvan dominated much of Cornouaille and Poher at this time, with his heartland around Le Faouët and the river Ellé. Louis attempted negotiation with him at first, through the abbot Witchaire, possibly offering acknowledgment of his local position in return for tribute, but Morvan was having none of this. In 818, Louis sent an army, which was unsuccessful, and then came himself with large forces.

Ernold Le Noir, a contemporary who wrote a poem of Frankish propaganda in honour of Louis, praises the noble spirit and idealism of Morvan, but laments the wildness of the Bretons (*ferae more*) and their penchant for anarchy. He also describes the guerilla tactics they adopted - 'bella per angustos agitabant improba calles' (stirring up wicked war among the narrow defiles) – using the terrain to their advantage against superior numbers.

Eventually, however, Morvan was forced to withdraw to his fortified position, perhaps on the hill of Menez Morvan at Langonnet. After a siege, he was eventually killed during a sortie and his body then beheaded by the enemy.

## Wiomarc'h

If Louis thought this show of strength was the end of it, he was soon proved wrong. In the early 820s, he had to come back to Brittany to deal with another staunch Breton, Wiomarc'h. This chief of Domnonée was increasingly active against the Franks in the border zones, harrying the counts of Rennes and Nantes with his raids. Three military campaigns were required to subdue him. Louis eventually secured Wiomarc'h's surrender and must have assumed submission too, but the Breton was active again not long after – enough to provoke an old enemy, Lambert, the Count of Nantes, who finally killed him.

## Nominoë

These experiences with the doughty Bretons taught Louis that a different approach might produce better long-term results than indecisive shows of military strength. Around 831, he appointed Nominoë, a Breton from a noble family of Poher, as Count of Vannes and *missus imperatoris*, the 'representative' of the emperor, believing that a sympathetic Breton-speaking leader with his own sphere of influence and power would lead to greater peace and unity in Brittany, and provide indirect Frankish control. It is possible that the two men had become acquainted during Louis' meeting with the Abbot of Landévennec at Priziac in 818 (see p.56).

Louis' measure did bring a degree of stability to a land weary of invasion and destruction. The benefits of a period of retrenchment and rehabilitation were obvious, and Nominoë's role was to keep the peace and maintain control over civil and religious authorities. Nominoë remained loyal to Louis until the latter's death in 840, but this lull in hostilities with the Franks gave him plenty of time to foster Breton unity and his own position, perhaps with a view to throwing out the Carolingians once and for all. The fact that Nominoë was soon in armed conflict with

Nominoë

Louis' successor, Charles the Bald, lends credence to this view, although some modern historians refute it.

In-fighting and intrigues among the sons of Louis the Pious continued, as the Holy Roman Empire was split between them. From 843 Charles the Bald was nominally in control of the western part, called Francia Occidentalis, technically including all of Brittany. From now on it is perhaps appropriate to use the terms France and French to describe this scion of the Frankish empire and its people, anticipating the gradual development of its independent entity from this time onwards.

Nominoë began to press into the border zone of the Marches, in alliance with Lambert the Younger who sought to regain the power he had lost in Nantes when his father's position was given to someone else by Louis the Pious. This was an important connection between the Breton leader and his Gallic ally, strengthening Nominoë's determination to wrest the Marches from pro-Frankish hands. The *Annnales de Saint-Bertin* record Nominoë near Le Mans in 843, burning and pillaging before returning to his own lands to deal with Viking incursions.

The Bretons were now on the offensive, and in confident spirit. In 845, Charles the Bald led a large army into Brittany to deal with Nominoë, but he was decisively defeated in an engagement at Ballon (Bains-sur-Oust), where the Bretons employed new tactics, using the speed and agility of their horses to good effect against more heavily armed, less mobile foot-soldiers. When the French retreated into friendly territory, Nominoë pursued them as far as Anjou.

A treaty the following year confirmed Nominoë's power over his own lands, but he continued to attack the Counts of Rennes and Nantes, ever pushing at the eastern boundary. He also removed French-appointed bishops from their sees and replaced them with Bretons. He had already supported the foundation of a monastery by St-Convoion at Redon.

Nominoë died in 851, after laying the foundations for an independent Brittany. He remains a crucial figure in Breton history, still honoured today in an annual festival as Father of his Country (Tad ar Vro).

## Viking raids

The first blows of the Viking menace that would plague Brittany for the next hundred years were felt in this period.

In 843, Nantes was subject to a sudden and devastating attack. The unsuspecting inhabitants were celebrating the feast day of St-Jean when the invaders rampaged through the city. *The Chronicle of Nantes* records the horror: "they spared neither age nor sex, and cruelly slaughtered (bishop) Gohard who was celebrating solemn mass." The cathedral was burnt down after those taking refuge inside had been massacred. The Vikings then looted the city and went back to their ships laden with valuables and many captives.

Another illustration of the Viking threat is the building of the abbey at St-Philibert-le-Grand-Lieu, south of the Loire, for the monks from the vulnerable Noirmoutier peninsula. In 847 they were forced to flee from here too with the relics of their saint and on return they built a special crypt to enclose his stone sarcophagus.

St-Philibert-Le-Grand-Lieu

### Erispoë

After Nominoë's death, his son Erispoë continued the good fight against the French with a further decisive victory at Beslé on the Vilaine, using the proven tactics of refusing hand to hand confrontation and using their superb horsemanship to harry the enemy from all sides in lightning strikes and withdrawals. Over three days, the French suffered serious losses and Charles the Bald was forced to negotiate or risk further humiliation. Nothing in recent history suggested that the sheer energy and resilience of the Bretons would be beaten by military odds.

At a meeting at Angers late in 851, Charles acknowledged Erispoë's title to kingship in Brittany and autonomy in his kingdom. This was the first open manifestation of a trend towards independence gathering momentum from the 6th century onwards. Charles' position was weakened by the internal dissents of the Carolingians and the inroads on their territory by the Vikings. If Nominoë was morally the first king of Brittany, Erispoë was the first to get the crown on his head. There had also been an implicit approval of the dynastic principle in Charles' acceptance of father to son transition of power.

Erispoë's kingdom was extended to include Rennes and Nantes, formerly in the control of French border counts (and much fought over by the Bretons), and the territory of Retz, just south of the Loire. The latter was an important addition to Brittany, giving total command of the Loire estuary and salt revenues from the Bay of Bourgneuf. The borders of Erispoë's kingdom were thus roughly those of true Brittany (including Loire Atlantique) today.

For much of the rest of his relatively short reign, Erispoë was occupied by continuing struggles against the increasingly menacing Vikings, who sacked St-Brieuc in 855.

A proposal to bind the French and Breton royal houses by a marriage between Erispoë's daughter and a son of Charles' may have been responsible for Erispoë's sudden downfall. Whether jealousy of his dynastic position or genuine fear for the end of Breton independence was the motive, the first king of Brittany met a violent death in 857.

## Salomon

Erispoë was assassinated by his cousin Salomon, who had

**Salomon**

his own ambitions. During his subsequent reign, Brittany was to reach its widest extent, when, in 863, a new treaty with Charles the Bald gave Salomon the land 'entre deux eaux' (between the Mayenne and the Sarthe) and later the area around Avranches and the Cotentin peninsula.

In general Salomon achieved his successes through political skills and a series of treaties rather than military initiatives. He was prepared to ally himself with Charles' enemies (such as Charles' son Louis and Robert Le Fort, count of Anjou), without directly opposing the French king.

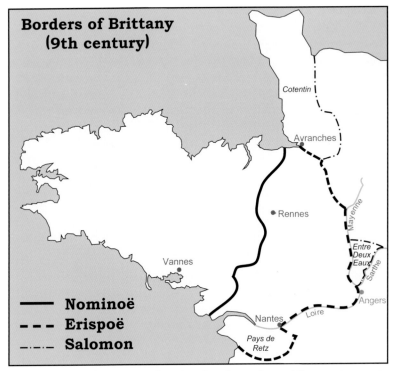

Borders of Brittany
(9th century)

Cotentin

Avranches

Rennes

Mayenne

Vannes

Entre
Deux
Eaux

Sarthe

Angers

Nantes

Loire

Pays de
Retz

—— **Nominoë**
- - - **Erispoë**
—·—·— **Salomon**

As king, Salomon maintained a luxurious itinerant court, and sent elaborate gifts to Popes Nicholas I and Adrian II, without managing to secure acknowledgment for the archbishopric of Dol which he had created. The Breton king also supported other religious establishments such as an abbey at Plélan for monks from Redon who were anxious to move inland to escape the threat of the Vikings.

He helped Charles the Bald against the Vikings near Angers in 874 but later in the same year, Salomon was assassinated by his son-in-law Pascwiten and Gurvand, the son-in-law of Erispoë. Albert Le Grand's 17th century *Life of Salomon* says that he had retired from public life after the death of his wife to devote himself to contemplation and prayer, and that his murderers had seized him at his retreat. The deed took place either at Plélan or, according to stronger traditions, after he escaped from there and reached a monastery at La Martyre (Ar Merzer) in Finistère, where the Church of Saint-Salomon now retains one of the oldest parish closes.

## Chaos

In the absence of a single strong leader, the following years were characterised by constant rivalries and disputes among the Breton nobles, who were not averse to appealing for French help to support their individual causes. There was also an increasing threat from the Viking attacks, which were not limited to coastal raids like that on the Ile de Batz in 884. Redon was attacked in 868, Rennes in 875 and Tréguier in 880.

Alliances of Breton nobles against each other and outside forces were complex and ever-changing, in the tradition of old Celtic tribal society. Pascwiten went so far as to ally himself with the Viking invaders in pursuit of sole power and made an attack on Rennes. He was beaten by Gurvand at the gates of the Abbey of St-Melaine, but both were killed in the battle within a short time.

## Alain the Great

They were succeeded by Alain and Judicaël, who united against the Vikings and pursued them with determination. Judicaël was killed, but Alain won a great victory at Questembert (near Vannes) in 888 and drove them out. Now undisputed leader of Brittany, he was given the epithet 'The Great' for this achievement, and Brittany was freed of their menace for the rest of his reign.

Alain was a staunch supporter of centres of learning such as the abbey of Landévennec and that of Redon. His own château was at Rieux, near Redon, although both Vannes and Nantes were capitals of his territory.

His reign marked the end of the short-lived kingdom of Brittany.

## Vikings

When Alain died in 907 (apparently without heir), another period of disunity and the worst of the Viking incursions ensued. Breton nobles again vied for supremacy, and the lack of leadership and united purpose allowed the Viking invaders to take advantage of a weakened Brittany. Whilst earlier raids had been bought off with gold, the Vikings of the 10th century looked more inclined to find land for settlement, and many Breton nobles left the area altogether, taking refuge in French territories or even England. The peasants, without choice or protection, stayed on their land for better or worse.

Monasteries with their well-known wealth were obvious targets for the invaders. The Abbey of Landévennec was destroyed in 913 and Nantes left in ruins once more in 919. At this time many monks also fled from Brittany, attempting to hide or carry away precious saints' relics and books, but much was lost or burnt and pillaged. The emigrations, albeit mostly temporary, were a crucial loss to Brittany, with consequences for the future of the Breton language and cultural identity.

## Alain Barbetorte

Jean, abbot of Landévennec, was one of the refugees after the Viking attack in 913. Aware of the need for another leader of stature to rally the remaining Bretons and end the Viking menace once and for all, he saw the potential of Alain (grandson of Alain the Great), who was currently in England. having been brought up at the court of King Athelstan. The young man was prepared to take up this challenge and the Saxon king (not disinterested in a Viking defeat) offered aid in the form of men and supplies.

Alain sailed for Brittany and gathered many supporters for his struggle. The Vikings had established a fortified camp inland at Péran near Plédran by about 930 and continued to cause havoc in the whole region. Various battles were fought - for example at Plourivo, where a stone

**Inside ramparts of Viking camp at Péran**

# ABBEY OF LANDÉVENNEC

(Musée de l'ancienne abbaye Landévennec)

The ruins of this prestigious establishment in their picturesque setting can be visited today. The abbey was founded c.485 by the monk Guénolé who had at first settled with his 11 followers on an inhospitable and barren island nearby. A later abbot, Gurdisten, writing in around 870 about the austere life of St-Guénolé, using an even earlier source by the monk Clement, says, "...In the middle of the island was a hill on which he used to sit with his disciples and talk. From here they could see a magnificent forest and hollowed from its midst a deep valley facing the rising sun.

Separating them from it there was, for a width of almost two miles, the open sea, into which flowed the river called the Aulne. From the bottom of the valley every day just after sunrise a mist rose like smoke, and to those who saw it the place seemed the most pleasant there ever was. They wanted nothing more than to be taken there."

In 818, in accordance with the decree of Frankish King Louis the Pious, the abbey adopted the Benedictine rule instead of that of the Celtic church. This was certainly a semi-political gesture on Louis' part, to eliminate Breton 'differences' from practice elsewhere in his empire.

St-Guénolé (Musée de l'ancienne abbaye Landévennec)

56

This development did, however, foster the growth of cultural activity and intellectual work, leading to the production of many fine illuminated manuscripts in the abbey's scriptorium. Examples of these, which include the subjects of medicine, grammar and astronomy as well as gospels and lives of saints, can be seen in the excellent museum at Landévennec. Whilst these were

written in Latin, some have marginal notes in old Breton, important evidence for the early use of this language. The Cartulaire (a collection of charters of land ownership), written in the 11th century, gives an idea of the vast lands on which the abbey's wealth was based, and the consequent importance of Landévennec over hundreds of years.

The fate of the abbey, in its vulnerable location, is a good example of these turbulent times. Archaeology has shown evidence of the fire which destroyed the abbey in the Viking raid of 913, and it was rebuilt before suffering much further damage in the turmoil of later political and religious conflict. Much of what remains now is from the medieval stage of reconstruction. A statue of St-Guénolé and the 'Tomb of King Gradlon' both probably from the 12th century are among the ruins.

An architect monk, Robert Plouvier, was in charge of more rebuilding in the mid-17th century, but his work was undone when the abbey was dissolved at the time of the French Revolution in the late 18th century. The cloister he had designed went to be used as part of the chicken market at Brest. The ruined abbey now fell into disuse until it was rescued by the Comte de Chalus in 1875. He began the process of examination and restoration which continues today. The Benedictine Order took over the abbey in the 1950s and built a new abbey higher up the hill: this is clearly visible across the water on the cornice road from Le Faou.

**15th century reliquary bust of St-Guénolé** (Musée de l'ancienne abbaye Landévennec)

cross from this period is said to commemorate the site of the encounter - and within a year Alain had established his supremacy, helped by Even, count of Léon along the northern coasts, and possibly Bérenger, count of Rennes, further east. A major victory was achieved at Trans-la-Forgêt near Dol in 939. (The *Annals of Flodoard*, however, claim that rivalry between Alain and Bérenger allowed the Vikings to sack Dol and kill the bishop there in 944.)

This virtually marked the end of the Viking invasions and the beginning of prosperous independence for Brittany. Alain ruled independently of the king of France, calling himself Duke of Brittany and not king, although he was sometimes given the name Ribret (or Roebre) which is a shortened form of 'King of the Bretons', an image possibly retained by the ordinary people.

Alain was both Count of Cornuaille (from his father) and Count of Nantes, but how much real power he wielded outside his inherited territories and in the lands of other Breton nobles is not known. The boundaries of Brittany were settled as they were in the time of Erispoë, including Rennes and Nantes, which became Alain's capital. He built a fortified residence there and rebuilt the cathedral.

Louis IV (king of France from 936-954) and Alain remained on terms of mutual respect, but the Breton court was increasingly Francophone. Many of the nobles who returned as the Viking threat ceased had acquired French influences and habitual use of the French language during their time of exile.

## Society

Social changes were inevitable as Brittany recovered from the ravages of the Vikings, and the ducal form of government became gradually established. The system was essentially feudal. At the top was the Duke, to whom other nobles were bound by oaths of loyalty and, as his vassals, obliged to support him with men and arms when required, in return for his protection of their rights and property. These nobles would also have their own less wealthy and powerful vassals, on similar terms, and so on, repeating the pattern of mutual dependency down the ranks. Fortified mottes (defensive mounds) surmounted by towers of wood and later stone were the strongholds of the nobles and the forerunners of the elaborate châteaux that remain today.

Peasants theoretically enjoyed the same security of protection from the lord to whom they were pledged, in return for various dues, including providing labour and paying taxes in money or kind. They did not own their land outright, but, because of the complexities of interdependence, the owner of the land they worked was not always the same lord who had the right to call on their manpower for war.

The Cartulaires of the Abbeys of Redon and Landévennec provide a remarkable range of detail of social and economic significance for this period from basic land-holding and material transactions to lists of lavish gifts given by named individuals.

### Death of Alain Barbetorte

Alain, whose later folklore epithets were Barbetorte and Al louarn (the fox), became ill and died in 952, leaving only one legitimate heir, whom he commended to the care of the bishops on his deathbed. The young man was assassinated some years later, however, leaving Alain's two surviving bastard sons to strive to retain their father's kingdom.

From the 9th century onwards, outside influences were inextricably fused with older Celtic traditions in Brittany, and the French language gained a hold, particularly in eastern Brittany, at the expense of Breton. The Viking invasions, with their dispersion of the indigenous nobility, put an end to Breton expansion and possibly to a developing unity of culture. The departure of the Vikings should have heralded a spell of much-needed recuperation, but in fact, Brittany was just at the start of a period of unparalleled turbulence.

# 5 - DUKES & A DUCHESS

After the death of Alain Barbetorte came hundreds of years of feuding and rivalry among the nobles within Brittany, and the constant outside intervention of the English and the French royal houses. Political marriages, shifting alliances, battles and bloodshed, territories gained and lost make this a complex period of constant flux.

## House of Rennes

The bastard sons of Alain Barbetorte could not consolidate their hold on power in Brittany. Tensions were strong between the counts of Rennes and Nantes who each regarded themselves as rightful dukes. Conan I, the son of Bérenger of Rennes, called himself the Duke of Brittany from 979. He was killed in battle in 992, but his son Geoffrey held onto the dukedom with the support of Richard, Duke of Normandy. In 1008, he was succeeded by Alain III, who managed to keep the count of Nantes under control, but had little success in shaking off Norman overlordship. He did, however, maintain his position for 32 years.

Conan II (duke from 1040-1066) became embroiled in armed conflict with his rivals, who now sought to use Norman power against him. Early scenes from the Bayeux Tapestry show William (the Conqueror) going to the aid of Rivalon versus Conan, who was forced to escape from Dol and flee back to Rennes, leaving William to take Dinan. The Normans, in the event, found the territory too hard-going and left without any consolidation of power there, but they maintained their influence.

**Conan escaping down a rope**
(from the Bayeux Tapestry)

Many Breton nobles fought with William at the Battle of Hastings in 1066, being later rewarded with lands in England. The Penthièvres, for example, from the area of Lamballe, were given the estate of Richmond in Yorkshire (although it later reverted to the English crown).

Conan II died without heir and was succeeded by his brother-in-law, Hoël, Count of Cornouaille.

## House of Cornouaille

Alain IV Fergent, Hoël's son and successor, was the last Duke to be Breton-speaking: in future the court would use French or Latin, a development which inevitably exacerbated the separation between leaders and people. During this period, the bastion of the Breton language retreated westwards.

In 1096, Alain went off for five years on the first crusade and retired to the monastery of Redon on his return. His son Conan III (1112-1148) continued the struggle for supremacy in Brittany in a period of unrest, which was to be taken advantage of by Henry II Plantagenet (king of England, also ruler of Anjou, Aquitaine, Normandy, Maine and Poitou).

## Plantagenets

Henry took an interest in controlling Brittany through Conan's grandson, who in England received the dukedom of Richmond, which had been his father's also, in return for allegiance to Henry. Once back in Brittany as Duke Conan IV (1156-1166), he had trouble in keeping control of the counts of Fougères, Léon and Penthièvre, and Henry was forced to come in person to reassert his authority. He took Fougères after a struggle and destroyed the castle. Archaeological excavations have found traces of a tower, which may be the one dismantled in 1166, on a rocky position within the current exceptional château

**Remaining tower base - Fougères**

site. Henry also destroyed the château at Josselin in 1168.

Henry used his time in Brittany to regularize administrative affairs, creating the office of seneschal to represent the duke in various regions.

He also organized the betrothal of his son Geoffrey to Conan's daughter Constance. By 1175, Geoffrey was in charge of Brittany. The earliest Breton legal document dates from one of his assizes, a decree forbidding the splitting up of the greatest nobles' estates among several sons – properties were to remain intact for the eldest. Geoffrey died in 1186 leaving a son, Arthur.

## French intervention

After Henry II's death in 1189, the king of France, Philippe Auguste, sought to undermine the influence of the kings of England across the channel. Henry had tried in 1183 to give his favourite son John (Lackland) some lands in France belonging to his brother Richard (the Lionheart). John wanted to establish his control here, but Philippe supported Arthur (Henry's grandson) as duke of Brittany and as lord of other lands in France, encouraging a collision course with his uncle John. In 1203 Arthur, in the process of besieging the castle of his grand-mother Eleanor of Aquitaine, was taken captive by John's soldiers and imprisoned. He later disappeared, murdered by John himself, or on his orders. But the English hold on French soil was fatally loosened through John's ineptitude and lack of decisive action.

## The House of Dreux

### Pierre de Dreux (Mauclerc)

The French king took advantage of this to expand his own power base. He turned to Alix, half-sister of Arthur, as the legitimate heir and married her to Pierre de Dreux, his cousin in the Capétien family. This far-reaching step meant that in 1213 the Duke of Brittany was of the royal French house and paid homage directly to the King of France.

Pierre de Dreux's period of rule was much occupied by the relationship between the duke of Brittany and the other Breton nobles. He strove to keep them in their place, fighting campaigns against those of Léon and Penthièvre, and attempted to consolidate his own ducal power by preventing others raising new defensive structures without his agreement. On the other hand, he needed their support

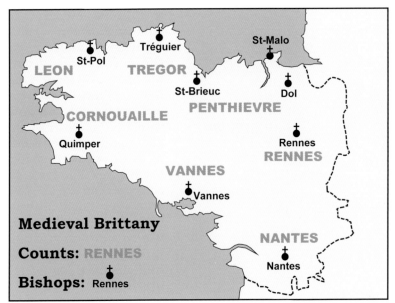

Medieval Brittany

Counts: RENNES

Bishops: ✝ Rennes

against outside interference: conflict and intrigues with both French and English kings continued. De Dreux improved the fortifications of Nantes, also developing the port there from which wine and salt were exported to England. He built a castle at Saint-Aubin-du-Cormier to keep a close eye on the eastern frontiers of Brittany, and this came in useful to repel the new French king Louis IX when he invaded after the duke's intrigues with the English king Henry III. In 1237, de Dreux passed the dukedom to his son and devoted himself to the crusades until his death in 1250.

### Father to son (1237-1341)

The dukedom succeeded directly from father to son in this period, without further serious dispute with the Kings of France.

Jean I (Le Roux)'s long reign (1237-1286) featured on-going disputes with the clergy and the expulsion of Jews from Brittany in 1240, in the anti-semitic climate then prevalent in Europe, fostered by the crusades and the raising of money for these expensive campaigns. He also took part in the crusades in 1270.

Jean II succeeded him, but his rule was cut short by a tragic accident. He left the Château of Suscinio in Morbihan

**Château de Suscinio**

in 1305, with an entourage of 86 people, including a fool, to see the coronation of the new pope, Clement V at Lyon. There, as he walked in procession with the king of France and the pope, a section of wall weakened by crowding spectators collapsed on them. The others were only slightly hurt, but Jean II died of his injuries two days later. His body was brought back for burial at Ploërmel.

His son Arthur II was duke from 1305-1312, followed by Jean III. The latter was the first to shed part of the de Dreux coat of arms and retain only the familiar black and white shield with ermine design for his own blazon.

**Blazon of Jean III**

## Wars of Succession

In 1341 Jean III died without an heir. Rival claimants to the Duchy of Brittany were Jean de Montfort (half-brother of Jean III) who was supported by Edward III, the king of England, and on the other side, Jeanne de Penthièvre (niece of Jean III) who was married to Charles de Blois, nephew of the then king of France, Philippe VI.

This war of the succession was to rage for more than twenty years and to see Brittany ravaged by marauding bands of soldiers (Breton, French and English), and great loss of life. It was fought in a long series of small engagements and alternating successes, with cities captured and re-captured by the rival factions.

Jean de Montfort first secured Nantes, but after a disastrous defeat there accepted safe conduct to Paris, where King Philippe imprisoned him in 1341. He was released in 1343 thanks to the energetic pursuit of his cause by his wife, Jeanne de Flandre after the Treaty of

Malestroit, imposed by papal envoys. The chronicler Jean Froissart (c.1333-1410) said she had the courage of a man and the heart of a lion, and describes how she rallied the troops during the long winter of her husband's absence. She earned the epithet Jeanne 'La Flamme' for her spirited defence of the castle at Hennebont.

The king of France's action of executing various Breton nobles, including Olivier de Clisson, for their support of the Montforts provoked further conflict. De Clisson's widow raised troops and equipped a pirate fleet to attack French ships. In 1344, Quimper was taken by Charles de Blois who allowed a bloody massacre of the inhabitants.

Jean de Montfort returned to Brittany with a supporting English force led by Thomas Dagworth, and they were victorious in their first battle, but de Monfort died before Quimper could be retaken. The English now dominated the territory and exploited their position for power and money.

They captured Charles de Blois himself in 1347 after a battle at La Roche-Derrien. Despite multiple wounds, he refused to surrender to Dagworth rather than a Breton, and was harshly treated, being kept captive in England for nine years before being released on payment of a huge ransom.

### Battle of the Thirty

Josselin castle was held by de Beaumanoir, who supported Charles de Blois, whilst nearby Ploërmel had a pro-Montfort English garrison led by Bemborough. In March 1351, an agreed engagement took place between the two sides. Thirty Breton/French knights led by de Beaumanoir faced an equal number made up mainly of English (with four Bretons and some German mercenaries) on the spot at Mi-Voie where today there stands a column commemorating this famous, but futile Battle of the Thirty. Graphic details of this 'example to encourage all knights' were noted with relish by Froissart, who actually

**Column commemorating the Thirty**

65

# BERTRAND DU GUESCLIN (1320-1380)

Bertrand du Guesclin grew up at Broons and became one of the most famous figures of medieval France. With his own band of soldiers, he supported the Penthièvres' claim to Brittany, and the power of the French throne against the English, achieving many remarkable successes in knightly tournaments and on the battlefield.

When his younger brother was dishonourably captured by the English knight, Thomas of Cantebury, during a truce at the siege of Rennes in 1356, du Guesclin took his complaint to the Duke of Lancaster at Dinan. There he agreed to fight a duel with the perpetrator to decide the issue. He was victorious in this combat, which was fought in the Place des Lices, where there is now a memorial stele. Du Guesclin went on to relieve the siege and save Rennes. Despite his valiant contribution at the crucial Battle of Auray in 1364, he was taken prisoner and later ransomed.

His achievements' were finally rewarded by the office of Commander-in-Chief of the French army, an honour conferred by Charles V, and he continued fighting in France and Spain for the rest of his life. He also has connections with the Château de Montmuran, where he married his second wife in 1374, six years before his death. Du Guesclin's bones were buried with those of the French kings at the Basilica of St-Denis near Paris, but his heart lies in the Church of St-Sauveur in Dinan.

met Yves Charruel, one of the battle scarred survivors, years later at the king's dinner table. All thirty knights were killed or wounded, but de Beaumanoir's side carried the day and 18 English prisoners were brought back to Josselin (and later ransomed).

## Montforts victorious

In 1362 another Jean (later IVth), son of de Montfort, returned to Brittany from the English court to take up his father's cause. The two sides met for a decisive engagement at Auray in 1364. Charles de Blois was killed in the battle and du Guesclin taken prisoner. Six months later, the French king, Charles V, acknowledged Jean IV as Duke of Brittany and accepted his homage.

By the Treaty of Guérande, the Montforts were to succeed to the duchy down the male line: if this ended, the duchy was to pass to the Penthièvres. The house of Penthièvre continued to foster the 'Cult' of Charles de Blois after his death. Pilgrims visited his tomb in Guingamp and many miracles were recorded. The pope, Urbain V, eventually agreed to his canonization.

The Montforts, finally victorious, could now consolidate their rule in Brittany, but this was not quite the end of the story. Jean IV intrigued against subsequent French kings and allied himself firmly with Edward III of England against the French. He was not particularly popular at home either. When du Guesclin entered Brittany at the head of a large army, Jean was forced to flee to England, until Charles V of France confiscated the Duchy of Brittany in 1378, which led to a clamouring for Jean to come back – the Bretons were naturally opposed to becoming subjects of the king of France. Jean finally renounced his English alliance, returned and made another treaty of homage in 1381 with the new king of France, Charles VI.

Jean IV built and improved many strongholds, such as those at Dinan, Suscinio and Clisson. His duchy signified a period of economic growth and prosperity, with flourishing overseas commerce with Spain, England and northern Europe. He also created a war fleet, but did not manage to subdue the recalcitrant citizens of St-Malo, who preferred allegiance to the French king Charles VI to submission to the Montforts.

## 15th century

His son and successor Jean V (1399-1442) tried to maintain a policy of independence from both France and England, but was on good enough terms with Charles VII for St-Malo, now with special trading privileges, to be returned to the duke of Brittany. In 1420 Jean was kidnapped by the ever-resentful Penthièvres, and their estates were confiscated after his release four months later.

Nantes Cathedral

The building of the cathedral at Nantes began in this period, with Jean laying the first stone in 1434 (although it took another 450 years to finish).

His son François I, whose brother was later murdered in captivity in England, was crowned duke at Rennes cathedral in 1442, and was later succeeded by his other brother Pierre II (1450-1457). Pierre's wife Françoise d'Ambroise, 'La Bonne Duchesse', was a remarkable woman of great piety. Albert Le Grand describes how she retired into religious life after the death of her husband to avoid remarriage and the intrigues of Louis XI, when he came to the throne of France, with designs on Brittany.

The next duke was Arthur de Richemont (uncle of Pierre), a soldier of note, who had been born at the ducal Château

Arthur de Richemont

of Suscinio in 1393. Wounded at Agincourt, he later fought with Joan of Arc at Patay, and when the Hundred Years War between Britain and France ended in 1453, he was the successful general who finally drove the English out of Brittany and Normandy. He did not become Duke of Brittany until the age of 64 and then for only a year before his death (1457-1458).

An equestrian statue of Arthur in the Place de la Mairie in Vannes was left alone by the Germans during the occupation of WWII because Arthur was a symbol of struggle against the English.

### François II (1458-1488)

The rule of François II, Arthur's nephew, began with promise and prosperity. He founded the University of Nantes in 1460 and was responsible for large-scale development of the ducal château there, including rooms big enough for the Etats to meet. Tensions with the French king Louis XI increased over the years, from taking opposing sides in armed conflict to Louis' claim in 1480 to have bought the right to Brittany from the Penthièvres, who had no male heir at that time.

François II called the Etats de Bretagne to gain recognition for the rights of his daughters, Anne and Isabeau. He also sought support from Edward IV of England, the Austrian emperor and the Duc d'Orléans. This aroused the wrath of the Rohans and other leading Breton

**Ducal château, Nantes**

families who were furious to be overlooked: more and more nobles were now looking to France to secure their possessions and positions. They called in the French regent Anne de Beaujeu (Louis' daughter) against the duke and fighting broke out. Châteaubriant, Redon, Vannes and Ploërmel were all taken and Nantes besieged.

In 1488 the decisive battle took place at St-Aubin-du-Cormier where Duke François was defeated. The subsequent Treaty of Verger dictated that he could not marry his daughters off without the French king's consent. Breton cases could now be tried in Paris, and the King would keep cities taken in the campaign.

## Anne de Bretagne

François died months after this debacle and the advisors of the young duchess Anne, led by Philippe de Montauban, determined to marry her outside France to retain Brittany's independence. In December 1490 she married Maximilien of Austria by proxy, but was forced to retreat to Rennes, allowing Charles VIII, new king of France, to enter Nantes in solemn procession, with an army 50,000 strong. Much of eastern Brittany fell to French hands. The Austrian emperor was too busy with fighting in Flanders and Hungary to send any help to Anne and she eventually conceded to Charles' demand for marriage. The Etats supported this as the only way to avoid more war and further destruction in Brittany. Charles was claiming the right to Brittany, as purchased by Louis in 1480.

The previous marriages of both Anne and Charles were annulled by Pope Alexander VI and their wedding took place at Langeais in December 1491. In the marriage contract, Anne's title of duchess of Brittany was not mentioned and a clause stipulated that she was obliged to marry Charles' successor if he died without issue, the latter to ensure that Brittany did not slip out of French hands again.

Charles soon appointed a Frenchman as controller of finances in Brittany (1493) and many other officials were now French, although he did agree to retain traditional taxes and for Breton rights to be judged in Breton courts. French garrisons, however, remained in the main towns.

In 1498, however, Charles died suddenly (after banging his head on a low door lintel) without heirs, his five children with Anne having died in infancy. Anne soon took the

## ANNE DE BRETAGNE
### MOTTO 'TO MY LIFE'

Anne was born at Nantes in 1477 and brought up in that city where much later she had an elaborate marble tomb built for her parents in the cathedral. This monument was regarded by the writer Chateaubriand as the leading masterpiece of Catholic art in France. Her main residence remained in Nantes, but she also favoured the Château de l'Hermine in Vannes, Suscinio in Morbihan, Clisson in Loire-Atlantique, and at Rennes, the Logis des Ducs.

Her political life started in early childhood and was always remarkable: not only twice queen of France, but also the last hope for an independent Brittany. Until her death Anne administered her duchy directly. She appointed officials and kept in touch with municipalities, and an eye on local conflicts. Copies of a few of her succinct, even terse, letters survive – these were written in French, the language of the court: her education did not include Breton. She was also a patron of the arts, encouraging, for example, the writing of historian Pierre Le Baud and poet Jean Marot.

In the summer of 1505, she undertook the Tro Breizh, a pilgrimage of the seven archbishoprics of Brittany, praying for healing for her husband who was very ill. It was a good excuse to tour her duchy and she visited many other places

including Hennebont, Morlaix, Locronan, Guingamp and Dinan, welcomed everywhere as the remaining symbol of Brittany's liberty.

**Tomb of François II in Nantes Cathedral**

decisive step of giving the position of chancellor of Brittany to her old advisor, de Montauban. She then married the new king of France, Louis XII, in accordance with her original marriage agreement, in the chapel of the château at Nantes.

Anne was in a stronger position this time, however, confident in her position as Duchess of Brittany, popular there and not entirely without allies. The terms decided before the wedding were advantageous for the queen: in her lifetime she would be responsible for Brittany, and afterwards her second child was to inherit the duchy, a measure to keep this separate from the French crown, to which the Dauphin (first son of the King of France) would succeed. If Anne died before Louis he would only have an interest in Brittany for his lifetime and then it would revert to Anne's heirs.

## The loss of the Cordelière
Coastal raids were becoming increasingly troublesome at the end of Anne's reign, with Henry VIII's commander Edward Howard leading the English fleet. He sacked Le Conquet and pillaged the Crozon peninsula, before a fierce-fought encounter in the Rade de Brest in 1512. One of the finest ships in the Breton fleet was the Marie de la Cordelière, which had been built at Morlaix for Duchess Anne. Those on board were celebrating the festival of St-Laurent, totally unprepared for battle, when the English appeared. After a hard contest between about twenty ships on each side, the Cordelière was blown up by its own commander, Hervé de Portzmoguer, rather than submit to the English. Details of the encounter and a scale replica of the ship can be seen in the museum in the restored 14th century Tour Tanguy in Brest.

## Death of Anne of Brittany
In January 1514, Anne died and her body was buried in Paris, whilst the gold casket containing her heart was brought to Nantes. The casket disappeared in later years, only to reappear empty: it can now be seen in the Musée Dobrée in Nantes. At Anne's death, there was general mourning throughout Brittany. Of her eight children, only two daughters, Claude and Renée survived. With the death of Louis in 1515, a 15 year old girl was all that stood between Brittany and the grasping hand of the French monarchy.

# 6 - UNION & PROSPERITY

In 1506 Claude, aged 7, had been engaged to François of Angoulème, against her mother's wishes. Anne would have preferred Charles of Austria, again with a view to preserving Brittany's future independence, but Louis was determined. Claude and François were married in May 1514.

When Louis died in January 1515 (having married Mary Tudor, Henry VIII's sister months earlier), there was no direct heir. François became king of France and was given the duchy of Brittany by his wife, first for his lifetime and then in perpetuity (June 1515). Then Claude agreed that it would go to the Dauphin (eldest son of French king) and not the second son, thus tying Brittany irrevocably to France. Claude died in 1524 (aged 24) and François pressed for a declaration of loyalty by the Etats.

**Union with France**

In August 1532, at Vannes, the Etats finally agreed a perpetual union of the duchy of Brittany with France. They had little choice, without powerful allies or military resources to keep the French out, but also many Breton nobles had effectively chosen the French side in return for privileges and position. It was politically better to agree, on the condition that their ancient privileges were retained, than to be forced into submission by arms and endure the loss of these privileges. The terms of the Union confirmed that no new taxes were to be imposed on Brittany without the agreement of the Etats, that there was to be no military service for Bretons outside Brittany and that Bretons were to be tried by Breton courts. Representatives from the Etats were sent from Brittany to the French General Assembly, where they often acted in concert, conscious of representing Brittany as much as individual interests.

Up to 1789 the French king was represented in Brittany by a governor, whose role was to maintain order and to supervise the Etats. He would be chosen from the high Breton nobility or from French royal family connections.

# ENGLISH ASSAULT ON MORLAIX

**La Fontaine aux Anglais**

In 1522 sixty English ships, in reprisal for recent raids on Bristol by the corsaire Jean Coatalem, made a surprise attack on Morlaix at a time when many nobles were at a military review at Guingamp and most merchants were also absent from the city at a fair. Troops entering by stealth and in disguise burnt and pillaged much of the town. One story goes that a chambermaid in a house in Grand rue opened the cellar trap, through which many hapless English plunged, before she was cornered and forced to throw herself from an upper window.

The Count de Laval led the returning Morlaisiens, who were in time to catch some stragglers, still recovering from their exploits, and take their revenge. The name of a fountain, Fontaine aux Anglais, where the water is said to have run red with English blood, commemorates this event in Morlaix. Other places in the area, such as the Manoir de Lézireur, were also plundered on this raid, and measures were needed to protect the Bay of Morlaix from future such incursions. By 1544, the island Château du Taureau with a garrison of thirty men and strong fire-power dominated the approach. From the incident of 1522 comes the motto of Morlaix, a pun on its name. 'S'ils te mordent, mords les'! (If they bite you, bite them back.)

**Château de Taureau**

## Breton Parliament

In 1552 a Parliament was established by Henri II of France as the main court of justice in Brittany. It consisted of 16 Bretons and 16 non-Bretons, with the latter group supplying a president. In this way, direct French influence could be maintained. Parliament also had a right of remonstrance, allowing an appeal to the king against proposed new laws. Nantes and Rennes disputed the location of the Parliament: in 1561 Rennes was chosen (apparently on the flimsy basis of having better accommodation available for participants) and thus became the political centre of Brittany from then on. In 1581 it was decided that Parliament should have a fine new building, but it was to be many years before this was achieved.

## Wars of Religion

From 1589 to 1598 Brittany suffered the consequences of the Wars of Religion that dominated France in the second half of the 16th century. There had been little infiltration of Protestantism in Brittany, although supporters included some noble families such as the Rohans and Lavals, and the French king himself, Henri IV, was Protestant.

The governor of Brittany from 1582, Philippe de Lorraine, the staunchly Catholic Duc de Mercoeur, tried to set up a principality for himself with Nantes as capital. He wanted to root out Protestantism and enjoyed widespread support in this throughout Brittany. Parliament, however, held out for the king, with Rennes, Vitré and Brest remaining royalist.

This civil war in Brittany brought terrible suffering to the land and to ordinary people over a period of ten years. Again foreign intervention was a factor, with Spain supporting the Catholics, and England the Protestant King. In 1590, 7,000 Spaniards and 2,400 English landed in Brittany. The Spanish established a fortress at Roscanvel on the Crozon peninsula, but it was destroyed in 1594: the spot retains the name Pointe des Espagnols today.

The same year also saw a bid for independent republicanism by the town of St-Malo, after the royal garrison were killed by the inhabitants. The mood of this time is summed up in their motto: 'ni Français, ni Breton, Malouin suis' (I'm neither French nor Breton, but Malouin). The town remained independent for four years until they surrendered to the French king.

# GUY EDER DE LA FONTENELLE

Many brigands took advantage of the turmoil of this period to destroy and pillage the countryside for their own ends. Called a 'viper' by the governor of Brest and Ar Bleiz (the wolf) in popular parlance, La Fontenelle and his exploits have captured the imagination of Bretons for centuries.

Guy Eder de la Fontenelle's short but eventful life began in the region of St-Brieuc in 1572. After an abortive attempt at college in Paris, he sold his books and robe to buy a sword and dagger, turning brigand at the head of a band of ruthless young followers. He became the scourge of the Trégor, the Poher and finally Cornouaille after establishing a secure base on Tristan island at Douarnenez in 1595.

From here, he terrorised the inhabitants, destroying much of Penmarc'h and Pont-Croix, amongst many other places, killing and pillaging with pleasure and impunity. Such was the loss of life and destruction of buildings and land, that agriculture in the area suffered seriously. Managing to foil a concerted attempt by the peasants to dislodge him from his stronghold, he is said to have murdered 1,500 men in the process.

After this swift, savage career, he finally submitted to Henri IV in 1598, after the Wars of Religion were over. When the king initially wrote to him in a friendly fashion and confirmed his control over Tristan, it seemed possible that the infamous La Fontenelle might settle to the sober life of a country squire. He was soon accused of intrigues with the Spaniards, however, and official action became inevitable. Aged 29, he was finally executed in Paris in 1602, and his head taken back to Brittany to be exhibited in Rennes.

La Fontenelle was married to Marie de Chévoir, whom he had abducted from her home in Léon seven years earlier when she was only 12. The young woman apparently died of grief within a year of her husband, and later Breton songs record the devotion that had developed between them.

**Signatures of Guy Eder de la Fontenelle and Marie de Chévoir**

**End of civil war**

In 1590, peasants from Cornouaille mounted a concerted attack on Carhaix in their anger against the violence and destruction perpetrated by royalist nobles in the area. The same year saw the siege of the Château of Kerouzéré (see front cover), base of a group of nobles and their followers who also had taken the side of the king. Catholic opponents, including a huge crowd of peasants, failed in their first onslaught, but then used canon to breach the walls, destroying one of the four towers, and inflict a bloody revenge on the occupants.

Henri IV's conversion to Catholicism in 1593 and his subsequent arrival in Brittany led to the submission of the Duc de Mercoeur. In 1598 Henri signed the Edict of Nantes giving freedom of worship to Protestants. He also promised to uphold the 1532 treaty of union between Brittany and France.

The war did little to advance Protestantism in Brittany. In 1565 there had been 27 reform churches in Brittany, but by 1620 the number had dwindled to nine.

**Michel Le Nobletz**

After the Wars of Religion, it was time for a renewal of spiritual energy. Michel Le Nobletz, born in Plouguerneau in 1577, was a notable missionary among the poor in western Brittany. He adapted his methods to suit his audience by using the Breton language and simple pictorial representations of biblical stories (taolennou – painted on animal skin or wood). Renowned for his own austere life and pure devotion, he was responsible for a widespread rekindling of faith among the ordinary people. He was buried in Le Conquet.

**Parish Closes**

During the 16th and early 17th centuries, many parish closes were built, particularly in the Léon area of northern Finistère. Here the wealth from the linen trade and lucrative fairs was poured by communities into elaborate expressions of religious art and architecture, often in a spirit of rivalry among neighbouring communities.

The ensemble usually consisted of church, ossuary and calvary with a precinct wall featuring an ornate triumphal entranceway. Inside the church, sumptuous retables (altarpieces) celebrated the cults of the parish's patron saints. The carving and relief sculpture is often outstanding: at Guimiliau over 200 individualistic figures people the calvary with all aspects of human life and death.

Calvary at Guimiliau

## Ste-Anne d'Auray

One August evening in 1623, a peasant named Yves Nicolazic from Keranna had a silent vision of Saint Anne. A year later the image recurred, this time saying that she wanted an old chapel in her honour on this site rebuilt. Later she told the peasant where to dig up an antique statue buried in the earth since the 7th century. The bishop of Vannes examined the peasant and, convinced of his honesty and sincerity, gave his approval for the new foundation. The statue was badly damaged in the French Revolution and its charred remnants were encased in the base of a later replacement. Today the shrine of Ste-Anne d'Auray is one of the foremost Catholic sites in Brittany.

## Cardinal Richelieu

In 1626, Cardinal Richelieu, who was in charge of navigation and commerce for France, became governor of Brittany to give himself access to Breton ports. The Bretons wanted resources to protect commercial sea traffic and there was much development of naval defences during this period. Richelieu decreed in 1631 that Brest was to become a military port, as the magnificent natural harbour would form an important part of French defence strategy. Richelieu also set up seven administrative posts for marine issues, but these were opposed by the Etats, as against their privileges, and did not last long.

In 1632 the Etats complained to King Louis XIII about excessive French financial demands, an issue that was to dominate the coming years, and he promised to abide by the terms of the original union.

## Trade and exploration

Initially the union with France was a time of economic expansion and prosperity for Brittany. Large ports such as Nantes thrived: it was very much an international trading centre in the 16th century, with large numbers of Spanish, Dutch and Portuguese connections.

In 1670, the French minister Colbert gave Nantes a monopoly of ships returning from the West Indies, a crucial step in the steadily expanding wealth of this trading city. Wine, wheat and salt were all important exports of the area, with the latter cultivated widely from beds around Guérande.

Lorient was established in 1666 on the confluence of the Scorff and Blavet rivers as a centre for naval construction and a base for the French India Trading Company (Compagnie des Indes), which was to benefit enormously from the eastern spice and luxury trade. The town took its name from one of the first ships built there, the 1000 ton Le Soleil Orient, more commonly called L'Orient. Nearby Port Louis, rebuilt by Louis XIII from its origins as a Spanish fort, provided an outer protection for Lorient.

**Port Louis**

Smaller towns such as Landerneau on the Elorn estuary, its centre today still a parade of fine town houses from this period, and Morlaix thrived with the linen trade of Léon at its height. Other centres such as Quintin and Locronan also produced significant quantities of cloth and sail-cloth. These exports to England were so lucrative that the 'maisons anglaises' of the Monts d'Arrée area were probably so-called because the money that built them came from this trade. Holland and Spain were other important markets.

The instinctive sea-faring prowess of the Bretons was also manifest in the competitive exploration of the age. Jacques Cartier, from St-Malo, was given the task of finding new lands for commercial exploitation and possibly a new route to India and China via north America. After several voyages of exploration, he claimed the land of Canada in the name of the French king in 1534, before retiring to his house at Limoëlou, near Rothéneuf, where he died of the plague in 1557.

Northern ports such as St-Malo, Erquy and St-Pol were beginning to expand their cod-fishing activities in the Newfoundland area from as early as the 1520s, with many boats away for the six month trip. Off-shore fishing continued to provide a living and a varied diet for the coastal regions, with the sardine catch developing in southern waters. The Aulne was a prolific source of salmon, so important to Châteaulin that the fish features in the town's coat-of-arms.

Arms of Châteaulin

Inland, there was much deforestation for ship-building from the early 17th century, and an expansion of the cultivation of blé noir or sarrasin, which provided the staple diet of many Bretons. It produced a good yield even from poor soil and this abundance allowed a surplus of other grains to be exported. Increasing numbers of cattle were reared, with butter an important by-product.

The production of salt from the marshes around Guérande and the Bay of Bourgneuf escalated considerably during the 16th century. This commodity was much in demand for the seasoning and preservation of food, with export markets all over northern Europe. The gabelle (a word originally meaning tax, but later signifying a specific tax on salt) had been introduced in France in the 14th century when Brittany was an independent state, and the region retained its exemption under the terms of the Union.

This led to a lot of salt smuggling into France, where prices in neighbouring Anjou, for example, could be up to twenty times as great. Customs officers attempted to intercept this illegal traffic and many violent encounters took place on the tracks through woodland on the border.

Industry also continued to develop. Quarries thrived with the demand for building and decorative stone, such as the distinctive dark granite from Kersanton, whilst tanneries, forges and paper-mills had high demand for their wares. The building of market halls, such as those remaining from the 17th century at Plouescat and Le Faouët, and the many large-scale commercial fairs reflect the general economic prosperity of this period.

**Market Hall, Le Faouët**

## Struggles

The long reign of Louis XIV (1654-1715) exacerbated the struggle between Brittany and France. During the 17th century, the powerful French ministers Richelieu, Mazarin and Colbert all sought to undermine the independence and expropriate the resources of the region, whilst the Bretons clung on grimly to the terms of the 1532 Union treaty for what little practical protection it really afforded.

In 1655 the Breton Parliament finally had a new building by Louis XIII's architect, Salomon de Brosse, in Rennes. (As long

**Parliament building**

ago as 1609 Henri IV had agreed to levies being raised on wine and cider to foot the bill.) This building survived until 1994, when it was set on fire during a demonstration and subsequently required large-scale renovation.

Tussles with Louis XIV over financial demands also began that year. Those sent to argue Brittany's case with the king were exiled, although a huge payment soon secured their return. Minister Colbert's centralisation of power, his need for funds to finance French wars and building schemes which were of no benefit to Brittany, led to policies that wrecked the Breton economy, with no respect or concern for the consequences. The absolute monarch's resentment of Brittany's special privileges was also a factor in the relentless pressure that the French government now began to exert.

In 1661 Louis XIV himself visited Nantes, and asked for a 'gift' of four million livres in return for this joyous event. The Etats offered two and finally settled on three. The Sun King's habit of demanding these 'gifts' to get round the fact that no new taxes could be imposed without the Etats' agreement (according to the terms of Union in 1532) was increasing. In 1663 he asked for 2,500,000 livres, was offered 1,600,000 but got 1,800,000 eventually. In 1665 it was the same story all over again. The effect of this constant bargaining was a serious weakening of Brittany's financial resources, apart from a source of considerable resentment and ill-will. Colbert's proposal of a whole series of new taxes between 1670 and 1673 was the last straw.

These demands were now beginning to affect all levels of society and cause general unrest and dissatisfaction with the situation. The next hundred years, leading up to the French Revolution, were to reinforce the strength of Breton grievances with the spirit of change in France itself. But an outbreak of violent resentment closer to home was on the immediate horizon.

# 7 - UNREST & REVOLUTION

The extravagances of Louis XIV and an expensive war with Holland led to these excessive demands for taxation. In 1673 Colbert tried to impose taxes on tobacco and make stamped paper (1 sol a sheet) essential for all legal transactions – he did this without the consent of the Etats, contrary to the 1532 agreement. There were also rumours that the gabelle (salt tax) would be extended to Brittany.

## The revolt of 1675

Soon these measures, which provoked unrest elsewhere in France, were inflaming Brittany. At Nantes and Rennes the offices of paper-works and the tobacco industry were attacked and Madame de Sévigné describes how a street violin player who mocked the paper tax was put to death and his body quartered. Guingamp, Dinan and Vannes also saw demonstrations in what started as an urban manifestation.

By June 1674, the rebellion had reached Carhaix, Châteaulin and Douarnenez in the west. In Basse Bretagne, the Bonnets Rouges (red caps) who were mainly country-dwellers from the Poher district and Cornouaille, began a revolt in earnest in 1675. (In a letter of July 1675, Madame de Sévigné refers to them as 'Bonnets Bleus'.) A Breton song of the time ran 'What's new in Brittany? A lot of noise and smoke...'

The Château de Kergoat near St-Hernin was attacked by thousands of peasants and set on fire, a fate met by many other châteaux at this time. The surge of feeling was not just against the new taxes, but also general social abuses by the nobility. The publication of the Peasant Code (or 'Pezavat', a short version of the Breton meaning 'what is good') set out their demands for justice and an end to oppressive practices. Concarneau and Pont L'Abbé were both taken by the rebels during the initial momentum.

One leader of the Bonnets Rouges, former notaire

Sébastien Le Balp from Kergloff, aimed to secure Morlaix's port as a route for aid for the rebellion from the Dutch fleet in the Channel. He was murdered at Ty Meur near Poullaouen by the marquis de Montgaillard, possibly his prisoner, or someone he was hoping to persuade to contribute military experience for the inevitable battles ahead with government forces. Without a figurehead, resistance faltered.

The Duc de Chaulnes, governor of Brittany since 1669, was unable to get out of the fortress at Port-Louis until Colbert sent 6,000 men to Brittany to suppress the revolt, when he energetically pursued the insurgents. Reprisals by the troops were savage, with indiscriminate violence, torture and mass executions. At Combrit, where the local marquis had been killed, 14 peasants were hung from one oak tree. Bloody revenge was worst in Bigouden country around Pont L'Abbé, and churches there also had their bells – which had sounded the call to arms – destroyed. The church of Lambour, which has never been rebuilt, remains a stark reminder of these terrible events.

**Church of Lambour**

By February 1676, even the Duc de Chaulnes was writing that soldiers were treating Brittany like enemy territory, a sentiment echoed in the letters of Madame de Sévigné. Rennes was punished for its role in the uprising by the exile of Parliament to Vannes, where it continued until 1690. 10,000 soldiers were billeted on Rennes' inhabitants, whom they raped, murdered and robbed, according to the journal of a contemporary, René du Chemin.

The town was to suffer terrible hardship of another kind in 1720, when fire, raging for six days, destroyed much of the old centre, flames spreading easily between the wooden houses. Thousands of people were left homeless and a huge programme of reconstruction was necessary.

## MADAME DE SÉVIGNÉ
### (1626-1696)

Madame de Sévigné

*Born in Paris, she came to the Château des Rochers in Brittany by virtue of her marriage at the age of 18 to Henri de Sévigné. They had two children before her husband died as a result of a duel, and she never married again. On marriage, her beloved daughter went to live in Provence, and this separation led to an outpouring of affection through letters. Madame de Sévigné was also in correspondence with many*

Château des Rochers-Sévigné

*notable figures of the time and her observations provide an important source of information about contemporary events. The first published edition of letters appeared in 1734, long after her death.*

### Last years of the Ancienne Régime

Louis XIV died in 1715, to be succeeded by Louis XV (aged 5), with the Duke of Orleans as Regent. The Breton Parliament, which had lost the right of 'remonstrance' (appealing to the king against new laws) under Louis XIV, got it back after his death. The Etats continued to meet and still strove for the 1532 treaty to be respected by the French government.

Under the Ancienne Régime, Brittany was under the control of royal appointees. The Duc de Chaulnes was forced out in 1695, with the Comte de Toulouse becoming governor until 1737 and then Louis de Bourbon (Comte de Penthièvre) until 1789. To prevent too great an accretion of regional power by these men, the French king could also send an individual who represented him directly (intendant), and employ a Commander in Chief with a

# VAUBAN (1633-1707)

Sébastien Le Prestre de Vauban became royal engineer at the age of 22. He spent the rest of his life in service to the king, constantly travelling all over France to organize and oversee defensive works. His strategic stance involved concentrating resources on geographical strong points, aligning fortifications to the contours of the land.

In Brittany he has left much evidence of his military genius. Defensive plans for the rade of Brest included the Fort de Bertheaume and works at Camaret, where he chose the distinctively coloured bricks for the Tour Vauban. This played a crucial role in fending off an Anglo-Dutch attack in 1694. He also planned many installations at St-Malo, designed the Citadel Vauban on Belle-Ile, largest of the Breton islands, and improved the defence of Concarneau. He was also responsible for the first lighthouse in Brittany on the island of Ouessant.

**Tour Vauban, Camaret**

Known for his honesty and modesty, Vauban was also the author of many written works on engineering and other subjects as diverse as forestry, taxation and pig-breeding. Louis XIV gave him the rank of Marshal in 1703, but he fell from favour at the end of his life for his avid support of tolerance for the Protestant Huguenots.

military role, as access to the ports was always crucial to the security of France.

The work of Vauban indicated Brittany's defensive importance in strategic terms and the need for adequate fortification. France had declared war on England in 1744 and now had to counter the threat of the English navy. An English attack on Lorient in 1746 ended in debacle: 8,000 men successfully disembarked and encircled the town with gun batteries, but then gave up after a week and sailed off again. The Seven Years War (over colonial and foreign policy issues) began between the two nations in 1756. English troops under Charles Spencer, Duke of Marlborough, landed at Cancale in 1758 with the aim of destroying ships at St-Malo, but in the event they left after burning vessels at St-Servan. In September of the same year, nearly 10,000 English troops landed at St-Briac for another attempt on St-Malo. A week later they

**Monument at St-Cast**

were re-embarking at St-Cast-Le-Guildo when they were attacked, at first by a small group of local forces, then by the Duc d'Aiguillon and his army. More than 2000 English were killed and 732 taken prisoner. The 149 Breton and French dead were buried there in what is now called the Cimetière des Braves. A column at St-Cast showing the greyhound (Brittany) triumphing over the leopard (England) commemorates the battle.

## Conspiracy

Fuelled by the struggles of the Etats and Parliament against the loss of Breton privileges sanctioned in the 1532 treaty, the year 1720 saw a conspiracy of minor Breton nobles and their followers. They hoped to win the support of Philip V of Spain for an attempt against the French royal house, possibly hoping to ensure Brittany's independence once again if successful. There was no widespread support and the leaders were eventually arrested. The Marquis de Pontcallec was betrayed by a friend. All four captured conspirators were tried, convicted and executed on the same day, 4th May, in the Place du Bouffay, Nantes.

## Trade and ports

After initial development in the early years of union, Brittany's economy was beginning to suffer mixed fortunes, unhelped by constant European wars. During the 18th century, Nantes rose to become the second port in France after Bordeaux. Much of the wealth pouring into the city now came from the slave-trade. Ships which left Nantes with cargoes of weapons, fabric and cheap goods went first to Africa to exchange these for slaves and then to the West Indies to off-load this cheap labour and fill up with sugar and coffee for the return journey to Brittany. The fine 18th century architecture of merchants' houses in Nantes was built with the proceeds of this 'triangular trade'.

The Malouin corsaires (those with official permission to 'course' the enemy) energetically harried Dutch, English and Spanish ships in the Channel and further afield, protecting vital trading routes for France and taking many hundreds of foreign ships in their remarkable careers. René Duguay-Trouin (1673 -1736) had his greatest success at Rio de Janeiro in 1711 and was enobled by Louis XIV, whilst Robert Surcouf (1773-1827) famously ranged the Indian Ocean a century later.

**René Duguay-Trouin**

Economically, however, St-Malo, suffered something of a decline from 1720, when Lorient was still enjoying a monopoly of the eastern trade, but the latter became a military port after the demise of the French India Trading Company in 1769.

**Brest**

Ship building at Nantes and St-Nazaire remained important, whilst from 1680 Brest was a great military port. The Arsenal there had 5,000 workers before the Revolution, in addition to the naval base.

The bottom had been knocked out of the Breton linen trade by Colbert's swingeing increases in duties on imported English linen and the restriction of its entry to ports outside Brittany. In return England boycotted Breton linen from 1678-1685. Breton deputies appealed to the king in vain against this destruction of their commerce, and it was never to recover fully from the blow. Consequences for the region of Léon were severe, but trade in fine linen and hemp from the Quintin area continued, with sail cloth from Rennes and Vitré fulfilling the demands of the French navy.

The tobacco trade flourished in Morlaix, with factories established along the river in 1736. 25,000 hundredweight a year was produced just before the Revolution and 750 people were employed in 1788, in an enterprise which survived into recent times.

Tobacco warehouses, Morlaix

### Grievances

In addition to a progressive stagnancy in trade, peasant grievances against the nobles were increasing. Higher taxes and rents were demanded, and large areas of land once used by peasants were passed over to wealthier farmers. In much of Haute-Bretagne, peasants remained under the feudal system, whilst in Basse-Bretagne, the 'domain congéable' was a common system whereby the noble owned the land and the peasant the buildings, but the latter could not expand or improve facilities without permission from the owner (foncier), which was often refused. The gulf between better-off and poor was very wide in rural areas as well as in towns, and between those two environments there were often differences of tradition (oral or written) and language, with the Breton or Gallo (in Haute Bretagne) of the peasants and French of the urban dwellers.

## L'Affaire de Bretagne

In 1764, the Duc de Aiguillon, commander in chief in Brittany, came into conflict with La Chalotais, president of Parliament. The Breton Parliament was called to heel by Louis XV, but they refused to continue to function under these circumstances and Parliament was dissolved. La Chalotais was arrested and imprisoned in the Château du Taureau in the Bay of Morlaix, before being moved later to St-Malo. From his prison, he managed to publish memoirs, eloquently refuting charges against him. He was put on trial for inciting discontent in Brittany against the king, and, although no proof was found of his guilt, he and the other prisoners were sent into exile. The king endeavoured to impose a wall of silence around the whole affair. There was continuing resistance in Brittany from the Etats: eventually the Duc de Aiguillon was recognised to be the main source of the trouble and dismissed from his position in 1768.

In 1774 the new king, Louis XVI, freed Le Chalotais and restored all rights to Parliament.

## Arthur Young

On the eve of the French Revolution, the English agriculturalist and traveller Arthur Young was in Brittany. In his *Travels in France* (published 1792) he comments on the wildness of the country and its uncultured people. On entering Basse-Bretagne, he notes how, on first sight, the people appear completely distinct from the French, in language and appearance. Young was a staunch advocate of crop rotation, and urged growing turnips for animal feed instead of leaving land fallow. He was also in favour of land enclosure to develop the keeping of cattle and sheep. Early in the next century the Abbaye de Melleray was to experiment with 'English methods'.

## The French Revolution

### Early days

The time was ripe for major change as social conflicts, distrust and ill-will between the various orders came to a head. The bourgeoisie lacked the political power their economic importance warranted, and peasants were simply sick of struggle and abuse by their noble masters. There was good reason for widespread early support for the French Revolution in Brittany.

Some of the first blows were struck in Rennes. In January 1789 there were violent clashes between nobles and groups of young bourgeoisie. The writer Chateaubriand describes avoiding being trapped with a group of friends by breaking through the mob, sword in hand, in a bloody mêlée. Support for the revolution, as earlier for the American War of Independence, was also strong in Nantes. Almost immediately after the fall of the Bastille in Paris, the ducal château there was occupied.

In April, elections were held to choose 66 Breton deputies (2 tiers of bourgeoisie/peasants/low clergy). The nobles and high clergy refused to participate or to acknowledge the results. In Versailles and then Paris, the Club Breton was soon established as an important meeting place for deputies, who were known for their anti-nobility stance. On the 4th August, Guy Le Guen de Kerangall from Landivisiau made a powerful speech against nobility in the French Assembly. In the midst of this heady fervour, the Breton deputies yielded their region's special powers. Full of confidence and optimism for the brave new world of republicanism, they did not foresee the threat of centralization, or the possibly adverse consequences of 'equality'. It was a triumph of hope over experience in dealing with the French government. The Breton Parliament and Etats were abolished in November 1789.

On the 22nd December, France was divided into departments, with five established in Brittany: Côtes-du-Nord, Finistère, Morbihan, Ille-et-Vilaine and Loire Inferieure. The political structure of each was based on nine districts, subdivided into cantons and again into communes. Another consequence of this was to be the suppression of four Episcopal seats (Dol, St-Malo, Tréguier and St-Pol) so that there was only one bishopric per department.

## Sources of disquiet

In the elections of 1790, the peasants were at last able to vote for their own local officials, with the result that many clergy became mayors of their communities. Conditions of land-holding were not overturned, however, which remained a source of frustration to the poor in the countryside. Some châteaux were attacked by peasants, often with a view to destroying documentation of ownership. The Château de la Hunaudaye which was built c.1200, later

**Château de la Hunaudaye**

destroyed and rebuilt, was burnt down by Republicans and left in ruins. The National Guard did sometimes intervene against these marauding bands: some were killed, for example, at Sixt, near Redon.

Alarm bells really began to ring, however, as measures were passed in Paris suppressing the authority of the Pope. This left bishops answerable to archbishops only, and the new departmental dioceses caused protests in Brittany, still staunch in its Catholic faith, popular feeling running high in defence of the church and ministers – but worse was to follow.

In 1791 it was decreed that only clergy who swore the oath of allegiance to the new civil constitution could continue to practise. 75% of clergy in Brittany refused: in some areas of Basse-Bretagne, like Léon, the proportion was nearer 90%. Others who were prepared to declare their loyalty to the Republic were put in their place and given armed guards against the hostility of the people. Recusants were forced into hiding with support from their parishioners, and conducted ceremonies and rituals in secret. Resentment grew against the new bourgeois officials, who were pursuing priests keenly. This religious issue became the focus for growing anti-revolutionary feeling in Brittany.

There was further disenchantment when peasants began to understand that, in addition to the attacks on their faith, new taxes would be even higher than under the old régime, and new officials were every bit as bad as the nobles they had brought down. By the end of this eventful year, there was widespread support for counter-revolutionary measures. Unrest rippled through Morbihan, as peasants rallied to support their priests and bishop in Vannes in the face of a supposed threat to their safety.

## Bad news

Having started out with the noble intention of translating decrees into minority languages (which was done in Breton) the Paris administration soon back-tracked, perhaps overwhelmed by the extent of the task. By 1794 it was declaring that for a 'free people' there should be only one language, the same for all.

Peasants in Brittany under the domain congéable system finally became outright owners of their properties by decree of Assembly in 1792, but the measure was to last only until 1797 when landlords' rights were restored.

In January 1793 King Louis XVI was executed and the nobility's rights and privileges abolished. France was now under outside attack from Austria and Prussia. Initially volunteers were called for to defend the new Republic, but soon attempts were made to levy 300,000 men for the wars. When Brittany's old exemption was ignored, many peasants refused the call and began to arm themselves for other reasons. A strong rebel movement was also simmering further south in the Vendée. Soldiers were sent against all incipient rebellions and the counter-revolutionaries lost a crucial battle in October.

Federalists began to air their voice in Brittany, wanting to reduce the control of Paris over the regions and limit the power of the 'sans culottes' (urban poor) in the French assembly. Action was soon taken against these too and even against moderate Republicans, who could not condone the growing extremism of events in Paris.

Soldiers on the loose in Brittany after priests or opponents of the Republic committed many abuses against people and property at this time. The oak pillars of the market-hall at

# THE CHOUANS

There were signs of a counter-revolutionary movement in Brittany from as early as 1791, when the Association Bretonne was formed by the Marquis de la Rouërie near Antrain. This was an aristocratic, royalist group, but their plans to incite a wider rebellion were soon betrayed. The Marquis managed to escape before the soldiers from the National Guard of Rennes and St-Malo arrived at his château, but he died of a fever not long after in hiding at the Château de la Guyomarais in the Côtes-du-Nord.

The spirit of the movement, however, continued to spread westwards across Brittany. Many young men who refused conscription in 1793 formed armed bands geared to guerilla warfare. There was no general and concerted uprising, (although much activity during the Vendéen insurgence of 1793) but separate attacks on garrisons, convoys and targeted individuals.

The anti-revolutionaries were called Chouans, (after the cry of the screech owl -

**Pierre Guillemot**

chat huant - which was used as a signal). Each band had its own leader: amongst others, Sol de Grisolles, Pierre Guillemot and Georges Cadoudal operated in Morbihan, Jean Cottereau (often called simply Jean Chouan) around Vitré. Their symbol, used on embroidered squares sewn onto jackets,

was a red heart surmounted by a cross, sometimes with the words Dieu (et) le Roi (God and King). Support for the church was central to the movement: recusant priests often blessed the weapons of Chouan groups before they saw action.

1795 saw a daring raid on the gun-powder factory in Pont-de-Buis and a disastrous setback at Quiberon where a group of exiles with English support landed, hoping to incite all of western France to unite in rebellion. Their forces, however, were contained by General Hoche's troops on the narrow peninsula, with many taken prison and 750 executed. In this year Louis XVII, the young heir to the French throne and focus of royalist hopes, died of tuberculosis in the squalid conditions of his captivity.

Many others respected a temporary peace imposed by Hoche, the French commander, the following year, but when promises respecting the return of recusant priests were not honoured, Chouan groups revived and continued to operate. In 1800, they assassinated Audrein, Archbishop of Quimper on the road near Briec because he had voted for the death of Louis XVI.

Chouan activity continued well into the next century, until one by one the leaders were hunted down and executed. The Chouans are by no means forgotten today, with many memorials to martyrs of the movement and an enduring place for their exploits in Breton poetry and song. The Musée de la Chouannerie at Plouharnel on the Quiberon peninsula details the impetus for the movement and the individuals who gave their lives in its name.

**Portrait of a Chouan**
(Musée de la Chouannerie)

95

Plouescat, for example, were repeatedly slashed with axes and the cathedral at St-Brieuc was used for animals and weapon storage, its lavish furnishings destroyed.

## 1794

As the Terror took hold, 26 Breton federalists were condemned and summarily guillotined on 22 May 1794 at Brest.

In Nantes the brutality of the governor Carrier echoed Paris' tone. Several thousand inhabitants were shot or guillotined. They were perhaps the lucky ones. From the overcrowded prisons, rife with typhus, prisoners were taken at night to be sent out on barges, which were then sunk in the middle of the river. Several thousands 'royalists' died like this in the Loire between October 1793 and February 1794, hideous scenes recorded in later engravings.

## Napoleon

As the revolutionary movement began to implode in Paris, successful general of the French army Napoleon Bonaparte took advantage to stage a coup d'état on 10th November 1799, establishing his position as First Consul. Brittany welcomed the Concordat he signed with Pope Pius VII in 1801, signalling the end of persecution of the clergy. Those who had refused to take the Republican oath could now return - a triumph for the tenacity of peasants' support for the Catholic Church. Another significant decision was that, at least between 1800 and 1802, Bretons were once again exempt from conscription for fighting outside their region.

Napoleon gave General Brune 20,000 men and the task of seeing an end to unrest in Brittany and further Chouan activity. Peace must have seemed like a relief after the savagery of the Terror and the heart-felt struggle of the counter-revolutionaries in Brittany, but it was soon to turn to oppression once again, albeit in subtler form.

# 8 - WHITES & BLUES

The post-revolutionary period was a difficult one for Brittany. For the first time it was openly treated by the central administration as a region of France like any other. Privileges were lost, Breton culture and language came under threat, and economic hardship was rife in the first half of the 19th century. The Catholic church faced oppression, and ultimately the formal separation of Church and State. As government in France swung back and forth between monarchy, empire and republicanism, so the political divisions within Brittany developed.

This all lay ahead in the early years of the century, which saw almost the last throes of Chouannerie. After a royalist plot in 1804, Cadoudal was arrested and executed. The same fate met Guillemot the following year and Prigent in 1808. Armand de Chateaubriand, cousin of the famous writer, lasted only until 1809. Balzac was to write an atmospheric novel entitled *Les Chouans*, set in Fougères, twenty years later.

## Napoleon Emperor

Napoleon Bonaparte moved from First Consul to power as Emperor from 1804. In this year Pontivy was repackaged as Napoleonville, with fine new streets to be laid out, a huge

**Pontivy - Napoleonville**

97

square for military parades and public buildings worthy of this status. It was also to provide a military base for dealing with further insurrection in the Morbihan area. The changing name of this town is a good indication of the political swings of the century. When Napoleon abdicated in 1814 it became Pontivy again, only to change back briefly in 1815 on his brief return to power and then revert to Pontivy after the Battle of Waterloo. In 1852, when Napoleon III (nephew of Bonaparte) became emperor it was back to Napoleonville again and then another change in 1870 after the establishment of the Third Republic, after which it remained Pontivy. Napoleon intended to visit the town in 1808, after a stay in Nantes, but was intercepted at St-Nazaire by urgent business that called him back to Paris.

Despite brief interludes of peace, England was at war with France from 1793-1815, and the English blockade of Breton ports had a severe economic effect. Nantes was particularly hard hit, with its refineries bereft of raw sugar (cane), and St-Malo's fishing fleet had nowhere to go. A Napoleonic ship (Le Vétéran) was blockaded in harbour at Concarneau for three years. The textile industry continued to suffer and never fully recovered its overseas trade. This was a bad time for agriculture too, with a shortage of workers because of conscription. The exemption in accordance with old Breton privileges had only been observed from 1800-1802.

Under Napoleon, the administration of Brittany was regulated, with conformity and uniformity the order of the day, and regional individuality frowned upon. Officials, including local mayors, were appointed rather than elected, a significant step in relation to the Church, army and education system. Appointed Prefects had the main powers and they, like many bishops and teachers, were not Bretons. These appointees made clear the central government's hostility to traditional costumes, games and other manifestations of regional culture.

Active persecution of the Breton language also began here. A decree of 1793 had stipulated that throughout the new French Republic, teaching must be only in the French language. Standardisation was an obvious reason for this, but in Brittany the anti-cleric consequences of the measure seemed also an attempt to undermine the influence of the church. The widespread implications for Breton culture were clear, but as early as 1805 there were 'defensive' actions such as the formation of the 'Academie Celtique'. This was founded by Jacques Cambry, who was born in Lorient and had been an official at Quimperlé before going to Paris. In 1799 he had published *Voyage dans le department du Finistère*, a detailed work of observations on all aspects of life in the newly created administrative district. He also wrote a book, *Monuments Celtique*, reflecting growing interest in such areas of research.

## Political parties

The major political theme of this period, against the backdrop of frequently changing régimes in France itself, was the development and increasing polarisation of the two 'parties' – the Whites and the Blues.

The Whites were conservative and traditionalist, consisting mainly of clergy and nobles, opposed to the principles and practice of the Revolution. Peasants usually remained loyal to these, from faith or expediency. The strongholds of this political faction in Brittany were Léon, Morbihan, eastern Ille-et-Vilaine and Loire Inférieure.

On the other hand, the Blues were powerful in Trégor, Cornouaille, and Basse Loire. They were republicans, hostile to the nobility and the authority of church (including Catholic schools), and consisted essentially of the urban bourgeoisie and workers, although some of the poorest peasants, such as those living in penury in the Monts d'Arrée area, were also of this persuasion. But, as time went on, workers and their conditions were increasingly ignored by the bourgeoisie, even though their political views were loosely the same. In the second part of the century, workers began to look to socialism, and later communism, to improve their situation and protect their interests.

## The Restoration

In 1814, after Napoleon's imprisonment on the island of Elba, came the Restoration with Louis XVIII becoming King of France. He soon fled from Paris, however, on Napoleon's sudden return, only to come back after the French defeat at Waterloo and Bonaparte's final exile to St-Helena. Student demonstrations in Nantes and Rennes between 1816 and 1824 expressed the dissatisfaction that many felt at this return of the monarchy. Nevertheless, a column in memory

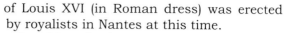

of Louis XVI (in Roman dress) was erected by royalists in Nantes at this time.

In 1824 Charles X succeeded Louis and held power until 1830 when another revolution in Paris forced his abdication. Louis-Philippe was then chosen as the 'Citizen King'. During this 'Monarchie de Juillet' new rules of suffrage, although still dependent on financial status, extended the vote far enough among the bourgeoisie to bring about a political swing to the Blues in Brittany.

From 1830 to 1832, small groups of remaining Chouans were active in the Morbihan area and the Duchess of Berry, Charles X's daughter-in-law, tried unsuccessfully to raise a rebellion against the new régime.

**Column of Louis XVI**

Her husband had been assassinated by those intending to wipe out the Bourbon dynasty, but the Duchess still had hopes of placing her son on the throne of France. After a disastrous defeat, she hid in a house in Nantes for five months before being arrested and imprisoned.

### The Second Republic

After a winter of terrible famine in Brittany in which thousands of people died, 1848 saw another revolution in Paris, with the king forced to abdicate and Louis Napoleon (nephew of Bonaparte) made President of the Second Republic. This year also saw the introduction of universal suffrage (for men), which favoured the whites in Brittany as most clergy and peasants still supported the conservative nobles.

### The Second Empire

In 1852, it was all change again when, under a new constitution, the President declared himself Emperor Napoleon III. Six years later he visited Brittany, dispensing largesse and going to the trouble of making a speech in Breton, which gained him popularity in the region.

Confrontations of Blues (in favour of democracy & progress) and Whites (for the preservation of rural life and Catholicism) characterised this period.

## Communications

The improvement and development of communications as the century progressed was instrumental in renewed economic growth. The vast engineering feats of the Nantes-Brest canal (finished in 1842) and the Ille-et-Rance canal (1843), conceived as strategic necessities in the face of English naval blockades, were never heavily exploited by industry, although building materials and agricultural goods were transported for a time.

**The start of the Nantes-Brest Canal near Port Launay**

The introduction of the railway network in Brittany came too close on the heels of the canals for the latter to prosper. From 1851 Nantes was part of the main French system, and by 1863, it extended as far as Quimper. On the northern route, Rennes had a station from 1857, and eight years later so did Brest. In the last years of the century a network of smaller routes took the train to ports like Douarnenez, resorts like Quiberon and the vegetable growing areas of Léon. In the west, Carhaix became the hub of many of these lesser routes (Le Réseau Breton), as it had been of Roman roads many centuries before.

As shipping got larger and larger, many smaller inland ports such as Morlaix, Redon and Quimper declined as

**Vitré Station**

St-Nazaire

they became inaccessible for this sort of traffic. St-Nazaire and Lorient on the other hand, developed into two of the most important ports in France. The increase in shipping and evolution of navigational aids were emphasised in this period by the construction of many lighthouses, including Les Heaux de Brehat (1840), Le Grand Phare d'Ile Vierge, the tallest in Europe at 82.5m (1845), Triagoz in the Bay of Lannion (1864) and Ar Men on the Ile de Sein (1881).

## Agriculture

Conditions in the countryside were poor in the early years of the 19th century, but then growth and development were to come. Generally more wheat and oats were produced, and less rye and maslin (mixture of wheat and rye). More and more land was devoted to potatoes, and vegetable growing increased with better communications and transport to wider markets. Léon was a notable region in this respect, producing large quantities of onions, artichokes and cauliflowers, whilst the strawberries for which Plougastel is still famous were cultivated in ever-greater numbers.

There were many seasons of crop failures, but the disastrous winter of 1847-8 saw a terrible crisis in Brittany, as both oat and potato harvests failed. Thousands died of starvation and disease, and desperation led to violence, including attacks on convoys of foodstuffs in Finistère.

From 1850 onwards, more and more land was coming into use for cultivation, which meant the loss of many wilder aspects of the landscape. Fertilizing materials (seaweed based) from coastal regions could be transported to the interior with new communications and this led to improved productivity. The extension of pasture land and growing of crops for animal feed resulted in greater numbers of pigs, horses and cows being reared. Brittany was one of the leading areas of France in this respect. There were also developments in farm machinery, such as the new design of plough with regulator called a *Charrue Dombasle*.

During the 19th century, however, the population of the countryside was decreasing and that of the towns increasing. Many migrants went to Paris, where there is to this day a large Breton community. The overall population of Brittany grew by a million in this period according to census figures. Some small towns, Loudéac and Josselin, for example, decreased, whilst larger ones like Quimper, Vannes and Rennes grew steadily.

**Industry**

In general, the 19th century saw the decline of traditional Breton industries. The linen trade, already struggling, later could not compete with the increased usage of cheap cotton. Lead mines in Poullaouen closed in 1863 and so did many iron foundries, although that at Hennebont thrived through providing for the expanding canning industry. This enjoyed something of a boom at this time, with tuna, sardines and vegetables conserved at ports like Douarnenez and Nantes. Quimper pottery, with its traditional colourful designs, remained popular within and outside the region.

Nantes remained the major industrial centre of Brittany, with metallurgy and chemicals, in addition to its food-processing plants. Ship-building also remained important there and especially at nearby St-Nazaire, one of the most important shipyards in France. Lorient too, since 1770 a military port, benefited from state investment in the development of steam and screw-propelled vessels as well as ironclad warships, such as the frigate La Couronne built in 1858. Arsenals continued to function at Brest, Lorient and Rennes.

The fishing industry saw a heavy concentration on the sardine in this period, but stocks eventually began to decline. In 1905 the famous Filets Bleus festival at Concarneau, now an annual event, began as a way of raising money to support the families of fishermen hard hit by loss of their trade.

## The Third Republic
The Second Empire of Napoleon III was only to last until the disastrous Franco-Prussian War, declared in 1870. Despite the best efforts of the minister of war, General Adolphe Le Flo, who is today honoured by a statue in his native Lesneven, Napoleon III suffered a series of defeats, and was forced to capitulate. After a revolt in Paris, the Third Republic was established just before the Prussian army arrived to besiege the capital. One of the French leaders, Gambetta, managed to escape by balloon and raised regional forces to attempt to relieve Paris.

A levy of 60,000 Bretons was stationed for months on the plateau of Conlie, near Le Mans. They endured terrible conditions and poor equipment because their loyalty was in question. In response to an enquiry from the mayor of Rennes, the Prefect of Ille-et-Vilaine replied that French leaders feared an 'army of Chouans' who could not be trusted. The troops were finally sent into the front line of battle, inadequately prepared, and many were massacred. This incident was the source of much anti-French feeling in Brittany, and the subject of an extraordinary poem by Morlaix poet Tristan Corbière.

## The Church
Many older churches - such as that at Ste-Anne d'Auray - were destroyed in this period to make room for larger edifices which still dominate numerous communes today. This confidence reflected the continued importance of the Catholic faith in Brittany, with the church remaining at the heart of rural life, especially in Basse-Bretagne. After the rebellion of the Bonnets Rouges and the religious issues of the Revolution and Chouannerie, the peasants clung as strongly as ever to this traditional security and spiritual focus of rights of passage. Annual *pardons* united the whole community and often attracted outside interest. These religious festivals devoted to the patron saint of a church combined mass with a ritual procession in which parish banners, relics and statues of saints were carried around the commune, with feasting, music and dancing to round off the day.

Cohesive as it was for the faithful, religion was, on the other hand, an issue of dispute in the growing divergence between town and country. It was also a factor for the

## TRISTAN CORBIÈRE
### (1845-1875)

Born at Ploujean near Morlaix in 1845, this unusual young man devoted much of his short adult life to his love of the sea, an obsession for Armida-Josefina Cuchiani, actress mistress of the Count de Battine and to poetry, largely inspired by their nebulous relationship. He made a trip to Italy with a painter friend in 1870, before the meeting that was to

**Father and son**

determine the course of his life. He then settled in Montmartre, Paris to be near the object of his passion. The ill-health which had dogged him since childhood finally forced a return to Brittany where he died, aged 30. He self-published Les Amours Jaunes in 1873, but it was the poet Verlaine's later recognition of his talent that gave Corbière his posthumous reputation. A library in Morlaix is named after his book, and he has a memorial plaque in the town.

'Allons donc: l'abattoir! – Bestiaux galeux qu'on rosse
On nous fournit aux Prussiens;
Et, nous voyant rouler plat sous les coups de crosse
Des Français aboyaient – Bon Chiens!'

from La Pastorale de Conlie

'Come on then – to the abattoir! Mangy beasts for beating,
Fodder for the Prussians;
The French baying 'Good Dogs'
As they see us rolled flat beneath the musket blows.'

His father Edouard, shown (left) on the plaque above, a sailor, businessman and journalist, was also the author of a maritime novel Le Négrier.

French government in political and educational developments. During the *Monarchie de Juillet* there were anti-religious moves in Haute Bretagne, with the Trappist monks at Melleray expelled in 1831 (to find another home in England) and a seminary at Vitré closed in the same year.

From 1870, the French government of the 3rd Republic took an increasingly anti-clerical stance. Many Catholic schools had opened in the 19th century and when some came under threat, the force of local protests required the intervention of troops.

The clergy of Basse-Bretagne remained staunch champions of the Breton language, closely associating it with their faith, and missions continued to keep the religious spirit alive among the masses. In 1902 their robust defence, backed by widespread public support, led to dropping of official attempts to stamp out the use of Breton in church services. A law formally separating Church and State was passed in 1905, however, resulting in further unrest and protest in Brittany.

**Tensions**
During the period between the Prussian debacle and the First World War, the movement of Breton identity gathered momentum, workers rights' became an economic and political issue, and Brittany began to develop as an attractive tourist destination, with resorts like Dinard, Morgat (on the Crozon peninsula) and Le Baule growing in size.

A law passed back in 1864 had given the right to strike, and this strengthened the growth of workers' movements in Brittany during the latter part of this progressive century. Agricultural labourers, fishermen and shipyard workers were amongst those to benefit from these organised groups. The 1890s saw the beginning of workers' unions in Nantes, St-Nazaire, Brest, Rennes and Fougères, for example, and there were to be more than 1,000 strikes between 1892 and the outbreak of the First World War. A general strike took place in Nantes in 1893, and in 1909 there were violent clashes during the conflict between cannery workers and factory owners in Concarneau.

Further important political developments saw the establishment of the Federation Socialiste de Bretagne in

Nantes in 1900, and the first PNB (Breton Nationalist Party) in 1911.

Reflecting the strong growth of interest in Breton folklore, songs and customs, the URB (Union régionaliste bretonne) was formed in 1898. The aims of this organization were primarily cultural. Their statutes outlined the scope of their interests, which were economic, scientific, literary, linguistic and artistic, and specifically excluded religion and politics.

---

## THE DREYFUS AFFAIR

*At the turn of the century, Brittany had a minor role to play in the famous Dreyfus case, when a Jewish French army officer was wrongly accused and convicted of treason. After many protests, including Emile Zola's article 'J'accuse', the case was re-opened. Dreyfus was brought from Devil's Island to a military prison in the rue Saint-Hélier, Rennes, in order to attend a second hearing before the Rennes military tribunal at the Lycée in August 1899. Feelings ran high in the town and Dreyfus' lawyer Labori was shot and wounded in the street. Dreyfus was found guilty again, a verdict overturned in 1904 when he was at last able to return to the army and resume his career.*

---

Overall, Brittany's fortunes were mixed in most areas during the 19th century, with vitality and progress in some areas matched by decline and repression in others. Absorbing struggles between the political factions and between workers and bosses side-lined and obscured the issue of the good of Brittany as a whole. Hopes for better things to come in the new century were soon overshadowed following the assassination of Archduke Ferdinand in Sarajevo in June 1914, which led to the outbreak of the First World War.

# 9 - WARS & BEYOND

The First World War began in August 1914. Bretons fought courageously in the army, navy and air-force, with a total of more than 130,000 lives lost, a higher percentage of participants than the French regional average. This perhaps reflects the still essentially rural nature of much of Brittany, as more peasants were called off the land to fight than factory workers. With both men and horses taken for war, women, children and the elderly rose to the challenge of maintaining food production in the fields, and there were also many female workers on production lines in the armament factories.

Foreigners poured into Brittany between 1914 and 1918: these were refugees, prisoners of war, foreign workers, and Americans forces. From June 1917, the latter arrived in large numbers in St-Nazaire and Brest, where a huge US transit camp was built just outside at Pontanézen. All this brought the Bretons into increased contact with other nationalities and cultures.

There are many moving war memorials paying tribute to those who lost their lives in the conflict. One of the most elaborate, dedicated in 1932 by the five dioceses of Brittany (Vannes, Quimper, St-Brieuc, Rennes and Nantes), can be seen at Ste-Anne d'Auray in Morbihan.

**War memorial, Ste-Anne d'Auray**

**Inter-war years**

The twenty years after the war saw a steady political conflict between left and right. The latter was still composed of aristocrats and clergy, now very influential and organized, controlling social clubs and sporting societies, as well as maintaining their influence in schools and agricultural syndicates. The Left was also adept at setting up alternative societies and cultural organizations, so some communes had two of everything.

In 1921 the first communist mayor in France, Sébastien Velly, was elected at Douarnenez, but such a large proportion of the Breton population was still rural (much greater proportionally than the rest of France) that conservatism mostly prevailed in elections. In 1924, the bishops of Brittany took the initiative for demonstrations against a radical/socialist cartel which came to power then.

During the inter-war period, despite increasing integration with French culture since the closer contacts of the war years, there were developing political and cultural movements for Breton nationalism, literature and language.

In 1926 Morvan Marchal (who 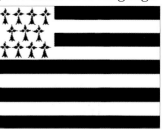 also had a strong interest in Druidic studies) designed the distinctive black and white (Gwenn ha Du) Breton flag, with its patriotic references to the days of ducal independence (ermines), the four episcopates of Basse-Bretagne (white bands) and five of Haute Bretagne (black bands). This later became the standard for certain political acts by the nationalists. A statue by Jean Boucher, outside the Hotel de Ville in Rennes, which commemorated the links between Brittany and France, was blown up in August 1932. It showed, among others, Anne de Bretagne kneeling at the feet of Charles, King of France.

The economic crisis of the 1930s led to strikes and social unrest in Brittany as elsewhere. In Nantes in 1933, there was a Hunger March (marche de la faim) to St-Nazaire involving more than 8,000 people.

There were some economic improvements during this time: motorized boats and refrigeration units on long-distance vessels helped the fishing industry, and, from

1936, state demands brought a revival of the ship-building industry. The aeronautic industry was developing at St-Nazaire and Nantes, and from 1932 there was a petrol refinery at Donges and metallurgy plants at St-Brieuc.

## 2nd World War

War broke out in September 1939, and this time brought occupation to Brittany. Between the 17th and 21st June, 1940 the German army took over the region, with three army corps totaling about 150,000 soldiers. 57,000 allied troops were evacuated from St-Nazaire and 32,000 from Brest, where the last British troops left on June 18, destroying port facilities as they went. The station at Rennes, packed with French and British troops and munitions, was bombed by the Germans, causing more than 2,000 deaths. German control of the ports at Brest and Lorient was secured as a matter of priority: the first U-boats were operating from Brest on August 22nd the same year. On September 27th, the RAF bombed Lorient, and numerous raids were to continue on Brest and St-Nazaire. Near Châteauneuf-du-Faou, the Château de Trévarez, used by the Germans, was also damaged by allied bombing.

From London at the end of June 1940, General de Gaulle, who had considered making Brittany the base for French resistance, made his emotional appeal ('Notre patrie est en péril de mort. Luttons tous pour la sauver!') for supporters for the Free French Army. Among many others, most of the able-bodied men from the island of Sein sailed in tiny fishing boats to join him in England.

In Finistère, it was at this time that German soldiers burst into the cliff-top home of the poet St-Pol-Roux, killing a servant, raping his daughter and

**Manoir de Coecilian**

injuring the old man himself. The ruined Manoir de Coecilian remains to this day above the beach of Pen Hat near Camaret.

The occupation of Brittany provoked strong resistance from mainly isolated groups. Numerous local memorials and street-names commemorate those who died in this way. After the Normandy landings, an armed Breton unit of the FFI (French Forces of the Interior), consisting of about 2,500 men, set up a camp near Malestroit covering more than 800 hectares, providing a safe area for allied parachutists to enter France. Defending their territory against a small German patrol on June 18th 1944, they could not prevent the escape of one man who raised the alarm and brought the enemy in large numbers. Battle continued at intervals throughout the day before a French withdrawal as darkness fell. Twenty-eight FFI members were killed, sixty wounded and fifteen captured. These events are commemorated not only by a monument, but also the exceptional Museum of the Resistance at St-Marcel nearby.

**Museum of the Resistance, St-Marcel**

This describes local resistance activities, and also presents a

111

detailed picture of all the deprivations, internal tensions and difficulties of life in occupied Brittany during the war, from realistic representations of rations to a tiny symbolic coffin delivered by resistors to those suspected of collaboration with the Germans. A few extreme Breton nationalists did try to gain their political goals through association with the Vichy government and the occupying forces.

The liberation of Brittany began from July 1944, with the Allies approaching via Rennes and St-Brieuc towards the stronghold of Brest. The siege here lasted until 18th September 1944, and there was still some German resistance in Lorient and St-Nazaire until the German surrender on the 8th May 1945.

Visual remains of the war still intrude along the coastlines with literally thousands of blockhouses forming the Germans' defensive Atlantic Wall. The Museum of the Battle of the Atlantique (the U-boat war) is housed in a German bunker at Pointe de Pen-hir on the cliffs near Camaret.

Atlantic Wall

## Post-War Years

The war wrought terrible destruction with the bombing of the ports of Brest, St-Malo, Lorient and St-Nazaire. Communications were in ruins, with bridges, roads, railway lines destroyed by sabotage or retreating German forces. Agricultural production was also hard hit, and the quality of agrarian life in Brittany was poor compared with the rest of France, despite the high percentage of the population working on the land.

The following years were of necessity ones of reconstruction. In 1950, CELIB (Comité d'études et de liaison des intérêts Bretons) was formed to bring investment and new factories into Brittany. Thanks to this organization and the Marshall Plan, money came into the region for improving agriculture and attracting industry, as well as repairing or developing communications. The suspension bridge over the Aulne at Térénez, for example, blown up by the retreating Germans to halt the Allied advance in 1944, was rebuilt and reopened in 1952.

There were also inevitable social consequences. Women were forcibly more independent, with about 30% left widows or single without an even chance of marriage. Many Bretons left Brittany after the war to settle in cities like Paris, or regions like Aquitaine where there was much fallow land to take over. For the same reason, Canada was a popular choice for émigrés. By contrast, in 1949 Edouard Leclerc opened his first shop from his front room in Landerneau, an enterprise which was to grow into the sizeable business empire it remains today, with supermarkets all over France and recent expansion into Italy.

In 1957 the department of Loire Inferieure changed its name to Loire Atlantique and became administratively the main region of Pays de la Loire. It had already been artificially separated from its historical roots as part of Brittany by the Vichy government in 1941, although it is both emotionally and routinely still regarded as such by Bretons today and work continues towards a reunification. It was also a great economic loss to Brittany being the only area with well-developed industry.

## Economic development

The years between 1960 and 1975 did see a growth of industry in the rest of Brittany, with companies like Citroën established at Rennes, Michelin at Vannes, and information technology giants Alcatel at Lannion. Service industries for agriculture (agro-alimentaires) also proliferated, although this hardly compensated for large losses of jobs in fishing and textiles.

Brittany was still the main fishing region of France, but in the face of problems such as distant fishing zones, costly equipment and maintenance and increasing foreign competition, numbers of fishermen dwindled from 20,000 soon after the war to fewer than 6,000 today.

Until the mid 1960s farms stayed small, almost at the level of subsistence farming without the benefit of modern machinery, but after the implementation of the Common Agricultural Policy, with greater economic security for farmers, more modern farm-buildings and greater production of crops, pork and chicken, were possible.

This transition to intensive farming led to the formation of many co-operatives and farming groups which encouraged investment. There were also the first signs of the radical action that was to increase as the century developed. In 1961, for example, the sub-prefecture in Morlaix was taken over, in a farmers' demonstration organised by Alexis Gourvennec.

New sources of energy were an issue now, with a site at Brennilis chosen in the 1950s for the first nuclear power station. Work began there in 1963, and a barrage on the Rance in 1967 helped generate electricity by tide power. By contrast, in 1969 the Armorican regional park was set up to preserve and foster the exceptional natural environments of western Brittany, from the island of Ouessant, via the Crozon peninsula and the Monts d'Arrée across central Finistère.

**In the Armorican regional park**

The UDB (Union démocratique bretonne) was started in Rennes in 1964 by a group of students and continues to work today for autonomy for a Brittany reunited with Loire Atlantique, a Breton parliament with executive powers and better representation for Breton social and political issues in France and Europe.

## 1970s
The 1970s were characterised by strong movements in the farming industry, with rapid modernization and increasingly common militant action by farmers. Alexis

Gourvennec set up Brittany Ferries in 1973, initially for the transport of produce to neighbouring celtic markets in Cornwall. By 1990 Brittany was to be the most productive agricultural area of France.

There was generally a marked increase in the political left in Brittany after the protest years of the late 60s, and by 1981 they were in the majority. Strikes such as those at Le Joint Français industrial material factories in St-Brieuc and the Doux abattoirs at Pedernec were common.

Militant Breton nationalism was also more apparent, with attacks on public buildings, such as that launched against the Monts d'Arrée transmitter in 1974. This was the work of the radical group the FLB (Front de liberation de la Bretagne).

Disaster struck the coast of Brittany in 1978 with the wreck of the Amoco Cadiz near Portsall in Finistère, spilling 227,000 tons of crude oil into the water, leaving 360kms of shoreline polluted, from Brest to St-Brieuc. One of the ship's anchors remains on the quay at Portsall as a reminder of the tragedy.

## Recent times

Large-scale demonstrations took place around Plogoff in 1980 during the public enquiry into use of a site on the Pointe du Raz for a second nuclear power station. The project was cancelled when Mitterand came to power in 1981. A documentary film called *Des Pierres contre des Fusils* was made during the protest by Nicole and Felix Le Garrec and songs describing events have entered the rich resource of Breton oral tradition. The existing plant at Brennilis was finally decommissioned in 1985, although work on dismantling the plant continues to this day.

The great storm of October 1987 made its mark on Brittany, with winds up to 200km/h causing widespread damage to trees, homes, agricultural hangars and boats, as well as electricity supplies. Over 50,000 hectares of forest were damaged or flattened. The forest at Huelgoat, for example, suffered badly, although replanting was swift and successful. Events such as this and the horrendous 'black seas' of oil spills did much to raise general environmental awareness in Brittany.

The Breton Cultural Institute was set up at Rennes in 1981, a source of initiatives for promoting all aspects of

# BRETON LANGUAGE

The Breton language is related to Cornish, Welsh, Manx, Irish and Gaelic and developed in Brittany from the time of British immigrations in the Dark Ages, probably revived from earlier Celtic dialects. The oldest manuscript in Breton (and Latin) is a botanical treatise dating from the end of the 8th century, from the University of Leyde in Holland. Other very early examples of old Breton are a manuscript from Redon Abbey dating from the year 821, and some marginal notes in Breton found in Latin manuscripts transcribed by monks. The Breton of the people, however, was largely an oral tradition, and had its stronghold in Basse-Bretagne, whilst French, Latin and Gallo were more common to the east.

In the medieval period, the first Breton/French/Latin dictionary appeared in 1499, and religious texts in Breton, such as that of a passion play, were published in the early 16th century. The foundations of modern Breton were helped by the work of Le Gonidec, who published the first Breton grammar in 1807 and a Breton dictionary in 1821. Not long after that, the publication of Villemarqué's Barzaz Breiz gave a voice to the Breton of the people.

Threatened for the last thousand years by the growth of French, which remained the language of administration, commerce and finance, Breton owes its survival through the centuries largely to the clergy and peasants of Basse-Bretagne. Many official attempts have been made to marginalise and devalue the language, and anyone with ambitions for a career in government service or the army would have had to speak and write in French.

From the time of the French Revolution onwards, the Breton language was persecuted by the central government. School inspectors in the 19th century, for example, exhorted teachers to punish children for speaking Breton. There was to be not a word of Breton spoken in the classroom or the playground. Pupils slipping into their native tongue were made to wear a humiliating symbol such as a sabot round their neck to mark their bad behaviour. The museum of the rural school at Trégarvan documents such attempts to suppress the language, which continued until the 1950s.

Estimated numbers of Breton-speakers in Basse-Bretagne dropped rapidly between 1900 (c.90%) and 1945 (75%), the result of hostility towards Breton in schools and an increasing contact with other nationalities through military activities and expanding communications.

After WWII, a law of 1951 (loi Deixonne) allowed the teaching of Breton at all levels, if suitable teachers and willing pupils were available, and in the 1960s Breton was 'permitted' on TV and radio.

Today, despite the many organisations and societies supporting the teaching and cultural spread of Breton, the number of those speaking it may be as low as 25%, some 240,000 people, although more may be able to read and understand at a basic level. As many of these are over the age of 50, rooting Breton firmly in a new generation has been a major aim of associations like Diwan which set up its first school at Lampaul-Ploudalmézeau in 1977 and a college in Brest ten years later.

In 1991 participants from all five Breton departments demonstrated in Quimper in support of recognition by French government for the work of Diwan schools as accepted regional language teaching. In another important initiative, the association Dastum is devoted to the collection of songs and traditions to preserve the essentials of Breton oral culture. Such work recognizes the crucial role of language in the continuing vitality of Brittany's unique identity.

**The bi-lingual road-signs which provide an outsider's first sight of Breton appeared in 1985**

Breton culture, which enjoyed a great flowering of interest throughout Brittany. This went hand in hand with renewed interest in the Breton language. The magazine ArMen, still essential reading today for Breton culture, was first published in 1986. Increasing numbers of books about Brittany were also produced in both French and Breton.

In the last twenty-five years there has been a marked increase in varied manifestation of confident and communicative Breton culture, which has aroused the interest and support of many other nationalities. Traditional music, song and dance, are widely performed (and taught), not for the entertainment of tourists, but as an articulate expression of ancestral skills and contemporary creation. The impressive vibrancy and extraordinary range of festivals testifies to this powerful cultural identity, from the huge pan-Celtic celebration at Lorient to the intimate festival of the violin at Plounéour-Menez, from formal concerts to the simple spontaneity of the fest-noz.

Workers' protests have remained equally energetic. A particularly virulent episode in 1994 led to the destruction of the Parliament building in Rennes, after it was set on fire by a stray firework during a fishermen's demonstration. Extensive restoration over years has been required to restore it to its former glory.

Another all too familiar catastrophe for the coastline occurred in December 1999 with the wreck of the petrol-tanker Erika, which broke in two off the southern coast of Brittany, having tried to reach St-Nazaire in difficulties. Four hundred kilometres of coastline, including the Vendée, suffered serious pollution.

On a more positive note, the development of tourism continued during the 1990s with initiatives to attract holiday-makers, particularly to the less well-known inland areas. A long campaign to change the name of the department Côtes du Nord to the more appealing and historically significant Côtes d'Armor was finally officially sanctioned in 1990.

From less than a million in the 1950s, numbers had risen to more than 8,000,000 annual visitors to Brittany in the 1990s. Coastal resorts remain the most popular destinations, but many themed sight-seeing routes, cycling, riding and walking trails, and inland waterways and lakes have helped the interior to widen its appeal as an attractive source of varied outdoor activities. Brittany remains as popular a holiday destination for French visitors as for foreigners.

Many of these projects have exploited the richly evocative vein of Breton legends, dipping into the shadowy world of korrigans and druids, magic and miracles, those endlessly fascinating resources of the celtic imagination which vivify the landscape.

The reality of Breton history is every bit as enthralling as the romance, if indeed such a distinction is possible or desirable. Whatever lies ahead in the 21st century for the Armorican peninsula, the experience of the past suggests that the resilient, resourceful and contumaciously indomitable Bretons will be more than a match for it. It is to be hoped that power over this future lies in the hands of the Bretons themselves.

# APPENDIX
## A Small Selection of Authors

### CHATEAUBRIAND (1768-1848)

François René de Chateaubriand, son of the Comte de Combourg, was born in St-Malo and spent his childhood there and at the Château de Combourg. In 1791 he travelled to America, which was later the setting for his first novel, an early example of literary romanticism. The horrific violence of the French Revolution drove him from France and he spent seven miserable years of exile in England, where he published his essay on the Revolution in 1797. Later works include *Les*  *Martyrs* (1809) a story of tragic love in 3rd century Rome and, at the end of his life, the autobiographical and lugubrious *Memoires d'Outre-Tomb* (1848). He was buried in accordance with his last wishes on the Ile de Grand Bé in the bay of St-Malo.

### LA VILLEMARQUE (1815-1895)

Théodore Hersart de La Villemarqué was born in Quimperlé. He studied in Paris, and travelled to Wales where he became interested in oral traditions of poetry. He later published his famous work *Barzaz-breiz*, a collection of orally transmitted Breton songs, poems and legends. Villemarqué sets out his methods in the introduction, describing his travels in Basse-Bretagne and participation in fairs, pardons and other community events to research his work. The authenticity of *Barzaz-breiz* was challenged on linguistic grounds, but later investigation and the discovery of his research notebooks appeared to vindicate the author.

### ARTHUR DE LA BORDERIE (1827-1901)
This great historian was born at Vitré. Early experience of working in the departmental archives at Nantes encouraged his interest in historical research. He founded and participated in many archaeological and historical societies, and was also politically active as Conseil-General of Ille-et-Vilaine and later deputy at Vitré. He published innumerable articles and books, including a major work on the history of Brittany, which was unfinished at his death but completed by a friend. La Borderie is buried at Rennes.

### ERNEST RENAN (1823-1892)
Born at Tréguier, Ernest Renan was one of the great thinkers of his time. From a staunchly Catholic background, he became disillusioned with the faith, which was undermined by his metaphysical and linguistic studies. A controversial work *The Life of Jesus* (1863) caused him to lose his professorial post at the College of France, but he was later reinstated. The extent of his research was prodigious and he published many works, including a monumental *History of the Origins of Christianity* and the more personal (and Brittany related) *Souvenirs d'enfance et de jeunesse* (1884). He is honoured today by a statue in his native town.

### ANATOLE LE BRAZ (1859-1929)
From Saint Servais in the then Cotes-du-Nord, Anatole Le Braz attended the lycee at St-Brieuc which now bears his name. He was a disciple of Renan and the folklorist François Luzel, and his work was an important factor in the late 19th century revival of interest in Breton legends and folklore. His method was to visit and talk with Bretons, especially peasants and sailors, collecting their memories, impressions and beliefs which he then translated from Breton to French in his remarkable work *La Légende de la Mort* (1893). Later works include the *Vieilles histoires du pays Breton* and a significant body of poetry. He also enjoyed a distinguished career as a lecturer in France and abroad.

Anatole Le Braz

la Légende de la Mort

coop BREIZH/JEANNE LAFFITTE

## JULES VERNE (1829-1905)

Jules Verne was born in Nantes, where a small museum (being renovated at the time of writing) is devoted to him. A prolific writer, fascinated by the world of science-fiction and the international language Esperanto, his best known work is *20,000 Leagues under the Sea*, which became a classic film. According to Anatole Le Braz, 'Le roman de Jules Verne, c'est l'air libre, c'est l'air vierge, c'est l'air irrespiré,' reflecting the breadth and originality of the writer's imagination.

## XAVIER GRALL (1930-1981)

Born in Landivisiau, Xavier Grall studied in Paris and worked there as a journalist for many years. He returned to Brittany in 1973 and settled near Pont-Aven, where there is a small memorial garden in his honour above the waters of the river. His writing evokes a deep love of the landscape of Brittany and a determination to give modern voice to traditional Breton culture. Passionate and forceful in both prose and poetry, his works include *Rituel Breton* (1965), *Rires et Pleurs de l'Aven* (1975) and *Solo* (1981).

## THEOPHILE-MALO CORRET - LA TOUR D'AUVERGNE (1743-1800)

Most famous for his exceptional military career, La Tour d'Auvergne, who was born near Carhaix, was also a man of great learning and intellectual curiosity. A descendant of Henri de la Tour d'Auvergne, he fought in the Wars of

American Independence and in Spain, before joining the Revolutionary armies in 1789. An heroic and committed soldier, he was later made 'Premier Grenadier de France' by Napoleon. In 1786 he published an historical account of Carhaix, and whilst a prisoner of war in England made good use of his time by writing a dictionary of French and Celtic languages. He was always a scholar of Breton and published *Recherches sur la langue, l'origine et l'antiquités des Celto-Bretons de l'Armorique* in 1796.

# SELECTED BIBLIOGRAPHY

The following is a selection of books which have been useful in research for this work.

*Histoire de Bretagne* - A. de la Borderie (1905)

*Histoire de Bretagne* - Henri Poisson/Jean-Pierre Le Mat (Coop Breizh 2000)

*Bretagne – une histoire* - Louis Elégoet (CRDP de Bretagne 1999)

*Nouvelle Histoire de Bretagne* - Georges Minois (1992)

*Les Origines de la Bretagne* - L.Fleuriot (1980)

*L'Armorique romaine* - Patrick Galliou (1983)

*La civitas des Osismes a l'époque Gallo-Romaine* - Louis Pape (Paris 1978)

*The British Settlement of Brittany* - Pierre-Roland Giot, Philippe Guigon, Bernard Merdrignac

*Le Finistère* - Direction: Yves Le Gallo (Bourdessoules 1991)

*Histoire de la Langue Bretonne* - Hervé Abalain

*Histoire des Institutions de la Bretagne* - M.Planiol (1982)

*Les rois de Bretagne: IVth-Xth siècle* - Philippe Tourault (Perrin 2005)

*Conomor: entre histoire et légende* - Christiane Kerboul-Vilhon (Keltia Graphic 2004)

*Les Bretons de Nominoë* - Jean-Christophe Cassard (2003)

*Anne de Bretagne* - Georges Minois (Fayard 1999)

*Anne de Bretagne* - Philippe Tourault (Perrin 1990)

*L'age d'or de la Bretagne* - Alain Croix (1993)

*Revolte du Papier Timbré* - Arthur de la Borderie (1884)

*Les Révoltes Bretonnes* - Yvon Garlan et Claude Nières (2004)

*Les paysans bretons au XIXe siècle* - Yann Brekilien (1966)

*La Bretagne: des Blancs et des Bleus (1815-1880)* - Michek Denis/Claude Geslin (2003)

*Le Mur de l'Atlantique* - Patrick Andersen (2002)

*Parlons du Breton* - Association Buhez (2001)

# INDEX

Some single references to people and places of limited significance are omitted. Places are followed by their department number.

Aber Wrac'h (29) 31,39,41
Alain the Great 54
Alain Barbetorte 55,58-60
Alain III 60
Alain IV Fergent 61
Alet (35) 28,35
Angers 47,51,53
Anne de Bretagne 69-72,109
Antrain (35) 94
Arthur, King 37
Arthur, Duke of Brittany 62
Arthur II 64
Arthur III 68-9
Auray (56) 66,67
Bains-sur-Oust (35) 50
Ballon (35) 50
Balzac 10,97
Barnenez (29) 21,22
Bayeux Tapestry 60
Bécherel (35) 29
Bemborough 65
Bérenger 58,60
Berry, Duchess of 100
Beslé (44) 51
Besné (44) 31
Bonnets Rouges 83-4,104
Bourbriac (22) 25
Brennilis (29) 20,114,115
Brest (29) 34,35,57,72,75,78,88,89,
    96,101,103,106,108,110,112,117
Broons (22) 66
Cadoudal, Georges 94,97
Caesar, Julius 9,27,29,30
Callac (22) 24,31
Camaret (29) 24,86,111,112
Cambry, Jacques 99
Cancale (35) 87
Cap Sizun (29) 39
Carentoir (56) 42
Carhaix-Plouguer (29) 30,31,32,34,
    43,77,83,101,122
Carnac (56) 15,20,21,24
Carrier, governor 96
Cartier, Jacques 80
Charlemagne, Holy Roman Emperor
    47,48
Charles the Bald 49-50,51,52
Charles VIII, King of France 70

Château de Combourg (35) 10,120
Château de la Hunaudaye (22) 92
Château de Kergoat (29) 83
Château de Kerouzéré (29)
    (front cover), 77
Château des Rochers (35) 85
Château de Suscinio (56) 63,67,68,
    71
Château de Trévarez (29) 110
Château du Taureau (29) 74,90
Châteaubriant (44) 70
Chateaubriand 10,71,91,97,120
Châteaulin (29) 80,83
Childebert, king of Franks 44,45,46
Chouans 94-5,96,97,100,104
Clisson (44) 65,71
Clovis, king of Franks 39,45-6
Colbert, French minister 79,81,82,
    83,84,89
Combrit (29) 84
Conan Meriadec 36
Conan I 60
Conan II 60-1
Conan III 61
Conan IV 61
Concarneau (29) 83,86,98,103,106
Conlie 104
Conomor 11,42-5,46
Corbière, Tristan 11,104,105
Coriosolites 26,30,35
Corseul (22) 8,30,31,32,33,35
Crec'h Quillé 18,20
Crozon peninsula (29) 72,75,106,
    114
Dagobert, king of Franks 47
Dagworth, Thomas 65
d'Aiguillon, Duc 87,90
de Beaumanoir 65,67
de Blois, Charles 64,65,67
de Chaulnes, Duc 9,84,85
de Gaulle, General 110
de La Borderie 121
de La Fontenelle, Guy Eder 76
de La Rouërie, Marquis 94
de Maupassant 10
de Montauban, Philippe 70,72
de Pontcallec, Marquis 87
de Sévigné, Madame 9,83,84,85

Dinan (22) 60,66,67,71,83
Dinard (35) 106
Dinéault (29) 32
Dol (35) 39,53,58,60,91
Donges (44) 110
Douarnenez (29) 33,37,83,101,103, 109
Dreyfus affair 107
Druids 27,29,40,109
Duguay-Trouin, René 88
Du Guesclin, Bertrand 66,67
Erispoë 51-2,58
Etats de Bretagne 69,70,73,78,82, 83,85,87,91
Fougères (35) 61,106
François I, Duke of Brittany 68
François II, Duke of Brittany 69-70, 71
François I, king of France 73
Froissart 9,65-6
Gavrinis 21
Geoffrey I 60
Geoffrey II, Duke of Brittany 62
Geoffrey of Monmouth 10,36
Gildas 35
Gourvennec, Alexis 114,115
Gradlon 36,37,57
Grall, Xavier 122
Gregory, Bishop of Tours 36,43
Guérande (44) 67,79,80
Guimiliau (29) 78
Guingamp (22) 35,67,71,74,83
Gurvand 53,54
Hennebont (56) 65,71,103
Henri II, king of France 75
Henri IV, king of France 75,76,77,82
Henry I, king of England 36
Henry II, king of England 61-2
Hogolo 33
Huelgoat (29) 28,37,115
Ile de Batz 41,54
Ile de Sein 102,110
Jean, Abbot of Landévennec 55
Jean I (Le Roux) 63
Jean II 63-4
Jean III 64
Jean de Montfort 64-5
Jean IV 67
Jean V 68
Jeanne de Penthièvre 64
Jeanne de Flandre (La Flamme) 64-5
John, King of England 62
Josselin (56) 62,65,67,103

Judicaël (1) 46-7
Judicaël (2) 54
Judual 44
Kerloas, menhir de 14,15
La Chalotais 90
La Martyre (29) 53
La Roche-Derrien (22) 65
La Torche (29) 18
La Tour d'Auvergne 122
La Villemarqué 116,120
Lamballe (22) 61
Lambert (elder), Count of Nantes 49
Lambert (younger) 50
Landerneau (29) 79,113
Landévennec, Abbaye de (29) 9,37, 41,49,54,55,56-7,59
Lanrivoaré 40
Le Balp, Sébastien 84
Le Baud, Pierre 10,47,71
Le Braz, Anatole 121,122
Leclerc, Edouard 113
Le Conquet (29) 72,77
Le Faouët (56) 48,81
Le Febvre, Yves 10
Le Flô, general 104
Le Grand, Albert 10,39,53,68
Le Mans 47,50,104
Le Nobletz, Michel 77
Le Noir, Ernold 10,48
Le Relecq (29) 44
Lesconil (29) 19
Lesneven (29) 9,32,42,104
Liscuis 21
Locmariaquer 23
Locronan (29) 71,79
Loire Atlantique 113,114
Lorient (56) 79,86,88,99,102,103, 110,112,118
Loudéac (22) 31,103
Louis the Pious, king of Franks 10, 48-50,56
Louis XII, king of France 72,73
Louis XIII 78,79,81
Louis XIV 81-2,83,85,86,88
Louis XV 85,90
Louis XVI 90,93,100
Louis-Philippe 100
Malestroit (56) 64,111
Mané Kerioned (56), dolmens 20
Marchal, Morvan 109
Maximus, Roman general 35,36
Melleray, Abbaye de (35) 90,106
Menez Bré (22) 29,39,44

Menez Morvan (56)  48
Mercoeur, Duc de  75,77
Merlin  37
Monts d'Arrée (29)  10,44,79,99,114,
  115
Morlaix (29)  31,71,72,74,79,84,89,
  101,105,114
Morvan  48
Mougau Bihan (29)  21
Namnètes  26
Nantes (44)  passim, espec. 32,50,68,
  69,71,79,87-8,96
Napoleon Bonaparte  96,97,99,122
Napoleon III  98,100,104
Nominoë  11,49-50
Osismes  26,30,34,43
Paimpont, Forest of (35)  37
Parliament  75,85,87,91
Pascwiten  53,54
Penmarc'h (29)  19,21,76
Pepin the Short, king of Franks  47
Philippe August, King of France  62
Pierre de Dreux  11,62-3
Pierre II, Duke of Brittany  68
Plédran (22)  55
Ploërmel (56)  64,65,70
Plogoff (29)  115
Plouescat (29)  81,96
Plouharnel (56)  95
Plourivo (22)  55,58
Plussulien (22)  16,17
Pont Crac'h (29)  31,41
Pont-Croix (29)  76
Pont-de-Buis (29)  95
Pont l'Abbé (29)  83,84
Pontivy (56)  97-8
Port-Louis (56)  79,84
Portsall (29)  20,115
Poullaouen (29)  31,84,103
Priziac (56)  49
Questembert (56)  54
Quiberon (56)  21,95,101
Quimper (29)  31,39,65,101,103,117
Quimperlé (29)  99,120
Quintin (22)  31,79,89
Redon (35)  53,54,70,101
Redon, Abbaye de  9,50,54,59,61,116
Renan, Ernest  121
Rennes (35)  passim, espec. 31,46,
  75,81,84,107,109,110,118
Richelieu, Cardinal  78,81
Riedones  26,30
Roche-aux-Fées (35)  18,19

Roland  47
Rothéneuf (35)  80
Salomon  52-53
Ste-Anne d'Auray (56)  11,78,104,
  108
St-Aubin-du-Cormier (35)  63,70
St-Brieuc  39
St-Brieuc (22)  35,39,52,96,110,112,
  115,121
St-Cast-Le-Guildo (22)  87
St-Conogan  39
St-Corentin  37,39
St-Gildas  42,44
St-Guénolé  37,56
St-Hervé  39
St-Just (35)  18,20,23,24
St-Malo  39
St-Malo (35)  39,48,67,68,75, 80,86,
  87,88,91,98,112,120
St-Marcel (56)  111
St-Nazaire (44)  89,98,102,103,106,
  108,109,110,112,118
St-Patern  39,42
St-Philibert-Le-Grand-Lieu (44)  51
St-Pol  39,41
St-Pol-de-Léon (29)  39,41,80,91
St-Pol-Roux  110
St-Renan (29)  24,31
St-Samson  39,44
St-Servan (35)  87
St-Tugdual  39
Surcouf, Robert  88
Tanoédou (22)  24
Térénez (29)  113
Trégarvan (29)  117
Tréguier (22)  39,54,91,121
Trémeur  44
Triphine  44
Tristan island (29)  76
Vannes (56)  passim, espec. 35,46,
  47,69,73,84
Vauban  86
Vénètes  26,30
Vernes, Jules  122
Vikings  50-1,52,53,54,58
Vitré (35)  75,89,94,106,121
Waroc  43,46
William the Conqueror  60,61
Wiomarc'h  48-9
Young, Arthur  90
Ys  37

## Rulers of Brittany
(mentioned in or significant to the text)

| | | | |
|---|---|---|---|
| Nominoë | 831-851 | Arthur | 1186-1203 |
| Erispoë | 851-857 | Pierre I (de Dreux) | 1213-1237 |
| Salomon | 857-874 | Jean I (Le Roux) | 1237-1286 |
| Alain Le Grand | 875-907 | Jean II | 1286-1305 |
| Alain Barbetorte | 937-952 | Arthur II | 1305-1312 |
| Conan I | 979-992 | Jean III | 1312-1341 |
| Geoffrey I | 992-1008 | Montforts | |
| Alain III | 1008-1040 | Jean IV | 1364-1399 |
| Conan II | 1040-1066 | Jean V | 1399-1442 |
| Hoël | 1066-1084 | François I | 1442-1450 |
| Alain IV Fergent | 1084-1112 | Pierre II | 1450-1457 |
| Conan III | 1112-1148 | Arthur III | 1457-1458 |
| Conan IV | 1156-1166 | François II | 1458-1488 |
| Geoffrey | c.1175-1186 | Anne | 1488-1514 |

## Kings of the Franks

| Merovingians | | Carolingians | |
|---|---|---|---|
| Clovis | 481-511 | Pepin the Short | 752-768 |
| Childebert | 511-558 | Charlemagne | 771-814 |
| Dagobert I | 629-639 | Louis the Pious | 814-840 |
| | | Charles the Bald | 840-877 |

## Kings of France

| Capétiens | | Louis XII | 1498-1515 |
|---|---|---|---|
| Philippe II Auguste | 1180-1223 | François I | 1515-1547 |
| Louis VIII | 1223-1226 | Henri II | 1547-1559 |
| Louis IX | 1226-1270 | François II | 1559-1560 |
| Philippe III | 1270-1285 | Charles IX | 1560-1574 |
| Philippe IV | 1285-1314 | Henri III | 1574-1589 |
| Louis X | 1314-1316 | | |
| Jean I | 1316-1316 | Bourbons | |
| Philippe V | 1316-1322 | Henri IV | 1589-1610 |
| Charles IV | 1322-1328 | Louis XIII | 1610-1643 |
| | | Louis XIV | 1643-1715 |
| House of Valois | | Louis XV | 1715-1774 |
| Philippe VI | 1328-1350 | Louis XVI | 1774-1793 |
| Jean II | 1350-1364 | (Louis XVII | 1793-1795) |
| Charles V | 1364-1380 | | |
| Charles VI | 1380-1422 | Restoration | |
| Charles VII | 1422-1461 | Louis XVIII | 1814-1823 |
| Louis XI | 1461-1483 | Charles X | 1824-1830 |
| Charles VIII | 1483-1498 | Louis Philippe | 1830-1848 |

**other RED DOG books**

## Finistère - Things to see and do at the End of The World

by Wendy Mewes

An introduction to this Breton department for visitors and new residents alike, through a series of tours taking in all the main places of interest and quite a few of the less well-known attractions that Finistère has to offer.

ISBN: 0 9536001 2 2      £8.99, 13.50 euros

## Walking Brittany

by Judy Smith

28 walks covering spectacular coast, hills and forests, varied water courses and traditional countryside. The text includes full directions and provides atmospheric accounts of places of interest on the routes - megalithic monuments, châteaux and sacred structures with their associated legends.

ISBN: 0 9536001 4 9      £9.95, 15.00 euros

## also by Wendy Mewes
## MOON GARDEN
## a novel

ISBN: 0 9536001 1 4      £7.99, 12.00 euros

www.reddogbooks.com